STICKY graphics

CREATE MEMORABLE GRAPHIC DESIGN USING
MNEMONICS AND VISUAL HOOKS

RotoVision

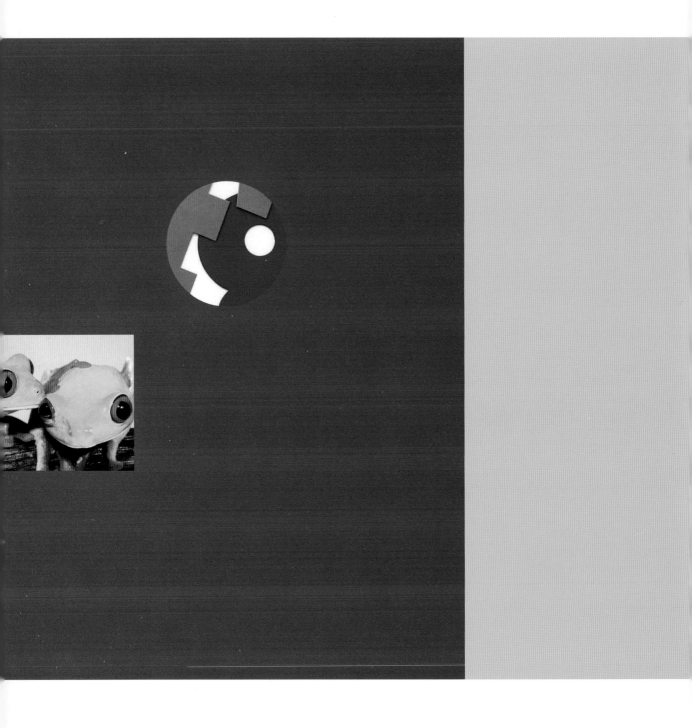
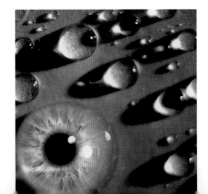

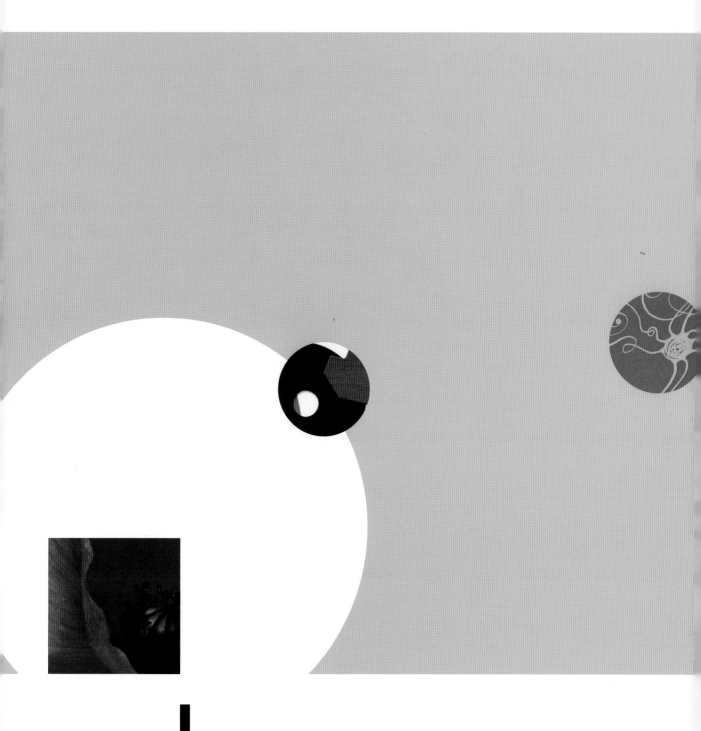

STICKY Graphics

CREATE MEMORABLE GRAPHIC DESIGN USING
MNEMONICS AND VISUAL HOOKS

CAROLYN KNIGHT & JESSICA GLASER

A RotoVision Book

Published and distributed by RotoVision SA
Route Suisse 9
CH-1295 Mies
Switzerland

RotoVision SA
Sales and Editorial Office
Sheridan House, 114 Western Road
Hove BN3 1DD, UK

Tel: +44 (0)1273 72 72 68
Fax: +44 (0)1273 72 72 69
www.rotovision.com

10 9 8 7 6 5 4 3 2 1

ISBN-10: 2-940361-26-6

ISBN-13: 978-2-940361-26-7

Design: Bright Pink
Additional photography: Calvey Taylor-Haw

Reprographics in Singapore by ProVision Pte.
Tel: +65 6334 7720
Fax: +65 6334 7721

Printed in China by Midas Printing International Limited

It would not have been possible to have written and produced *Sticky Graphics* without the valuable help and commitment of everyone who has contributed to its progress. Thanks must go to the group of international designers who have generously given their time and support, as well as allowing their work to be featured.

Special thanks must go to The School of Art and Design at The University of Wolverhampton, for constant interest and encouragement.

Lindy Dunlop and Tony Seddon at RotoVision cannot be omitted; their advice, assistance, and patience have been greatly appreciated.

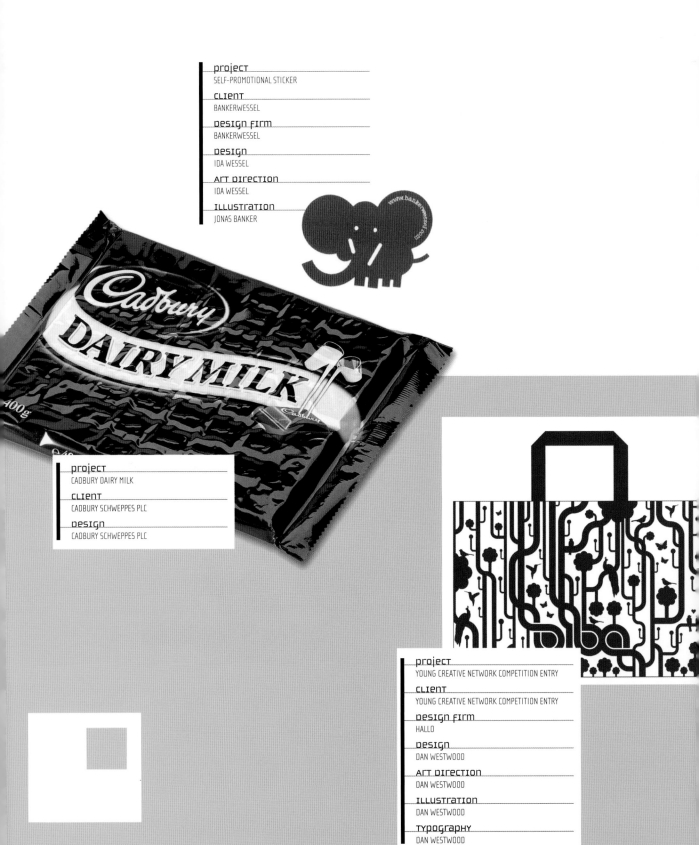

project
SELF-PROMOTIONAL STICKER

client
BANKERWESSEL

design firm
BANKERWESSEL

design
IDA WESSEL

art direction
IDA WESSEL

illustration
JONAS BANKER

project
CADBURY DAIRY MILK

client
CADBURY SCHWEPPES PLC

design
CADBURY SCHWEPPES PLC

project
YOUNG CREATIVE NETWORK COMPETITION ENTRY

client
YOUNG CREATIVE NETWORK COMPETITION ENTRY

design firm
HALLO

design
DAN WESTWOOD

art direction
DAN WESTWOOD

illustration
DAN WESTWOOD

typography
DAN WESTWOOD

contents

INTRODUCTION

Graphic designers tend to agree that their work should satisfy the criteria of both function and esthetics. In other words, visual and verbal messages should reach their intended audiences in a manner that is enticing, informative, appropriate, and pleasing. In addition, a third attribute is generally accepted: that a design should create a lasting impression on its audience. It could be argued that one of the primary challenges of contemporary graphics, in a world saturated with visual information, is to ensure that a design is memorable. Mnemonic devices are aids to memory that can be used in all kinds of situations to assist in the retention of any kind of information. *Sticky Graphics* explores the many ways in which design elements can act as visual mnemonics.

Visual memory is a fascinating subject; everyone uses it, both consciously and subconsciously, to help recall recent and more distant experiences. A simple test of this is to ask someone how many rooms they have in their home; most people will automatically walk through each one in their mind's eye, adding up as they go, before giving an answer. This phenomenon should not be overlooked or underestimated; graphic designers should tap into its benefits by providing visual triggers in their work that keep information fresh in an audience's mind. Professor Bruce Brown, Dean of the Faculty of Arts and Architecture at the UK's University of Brighton since 1989, has for a number of years focused his research on "graphic memory." In 1995, he said, "Despite the remarkable ability we possess to remember things, we take our memory systems for granted; alongside this we place little emphasis on the role of graphic images as the transformers of knowledge into memories and, subsequently, as the visual triggers needed to revive their dormant forms." *Sticky Graphics* aims to appreciate this role of the visual as a powerful aid to and creator of memory, discussing both design methodologies and solutions.

It would be impossible to definitively explain or describe a visual mnemonic: as with all design, general principles rather than absolute rules apply. However, it is safe to suggest that aspects of dynamism—the unexpected or the unusual—are likely to be featured in most memorable designs. Not all visual mnemonics are esthetically pleasing—very often, it is not their design quality that makes

project
CHILDREN'S CANDY

client
SOMERFIELD

design firm
TAXI STUDIO

design
KARL WILLS

typography
SPENCER BUCK

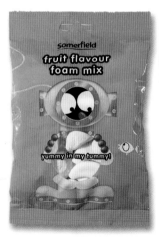

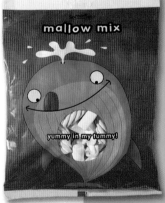

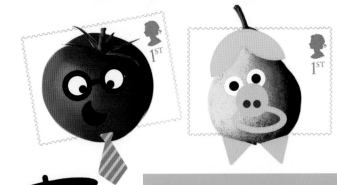

them memorable. Equally, just because a piece of work is beautifully considered and produced, it is not necessarily going to be remembered. A superb design might well be recalled, but with little or no retention of precisely how it looked, or what messages it conveyed. A visual mnemonic can remain in the memory as something to be recalled at will, possibly even in a personal rendition with a paper and pencil. A mnemonic can also be something that is immediately recognized at first sight, but requires a visual trigger to stimulate the viewer's memory.

A wide range of factors affect the chances of making a lasting impression. All design choices are relative, and although designers' skills must not be underestimated, very often an element of luck, particularly relating to context or timing, helps determine results. Conspicuous color relationships, shocking images, or clever type can be consciously selected, but whatever truly captures the viewers' imagination, and stays with them, is far less easy to define. Consequently, designers regularly create their own visual resources of striking and memorable work, in order to attempt to retain some of the most notable characteristics for future inspiration. *Sticky Graphics* brings together a contemporary collection of memorable design from around the world, discussing and analyzing the most mnemonically strong elements within each piece, and making for a fascinating and comprehensive source of stimulation for anyone interested in graphic design. There are four sections to this book: Color, image, and composition; Graphic wit and shock; Materials and processes; and Visual figures of speech. As the examples within this introduction demonstrate, work is taken from a wide spectrum of disciplines and locations, providing a wealth of memorable projects that intrigue, entertain, captivate, and inspire.

project
GREETINGS STAMPS

client
ROYAL MAIL

design firm
JOHNSON BANKS

design
MICHAEL JOHNSON

art direction
MICHAEL JOHNSON

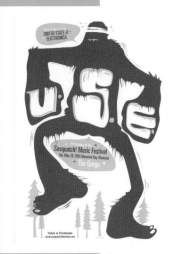

project
SASQUATCH MUSIC FESTIVAL

client
HOUSE OF BLUES CONCERTS

design firm
33RPM

design
ANDRIO ABERO

COLOr, Image, and COMPOSITION

Color, image, and composition have the ability to create visual mnemonics, both individually and collectively. They have been grouped together in this section because they are usually most effective in assisting memory when working together. For example, color combinations are frequently made more memorable through interesting shape configurations or contrasts of scale, whether they are used figuratively or in an abstract context. Even when colors have been deliberately selected for their optical or illusory impact, it is generally the manner in which they are used and composed that brings about memory retention.

Images possibly have the most potential as memory devices. However, despite shocking, unusual, or unexpected subject matter being comparatively noticeable, it is more likely that cropping, positioning, use of scale, and use of color in and around an image are what makes a design unforgettable. Comparisons of two versions of the same shot, one in a sensationalist tabloid newspaper and one in a supposedly more factual and upmarket newspaper, demonstrate that the large, closely cropped interpretation in the former is very difficult to forget. It focuses on the emotional, personal content of an event, and will not allow viewers to escape from the heart of what is happening. Conversely, the photograph that contains more contextual information keeps readers at a distance; although they may be just as interested in what is happening, they are less likely to remember what they have seen.

SECTION
01

Image and color can create strong mnemonics. Photographs that capture unusual or striking color relationships that are enhanced by momentary light in nature, or controlled lighting in a studio, often have a "wow" factor that is very memorable. When designers transpose accepted colors for unnatural or unexpected ones, this too can make an image stick in the memory—a blue daffodil, a green cloud, or a bright purple letterbox, for example, would grab attention, and are likely to be easily remembered. Relationships of simple images and colors, particularly within the context of branding, can take on iconic or symbolic roles that become nationally or even internationally known and remembered. Flooding the marketplace is bound to make these brands familiar to a vast spectrum of people, but considerably less publicized icons and symbols can also be remembered for their unique shapes and color combinations. Even typographic configurations that have distinctive shape and color come into this category, as they are recognized and remembered in a similar manner to images (see the display typography in Dan Westwood's magazine design on pages 28 and 29).

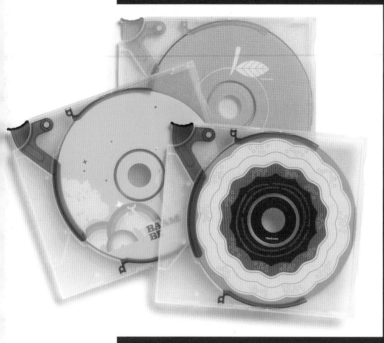

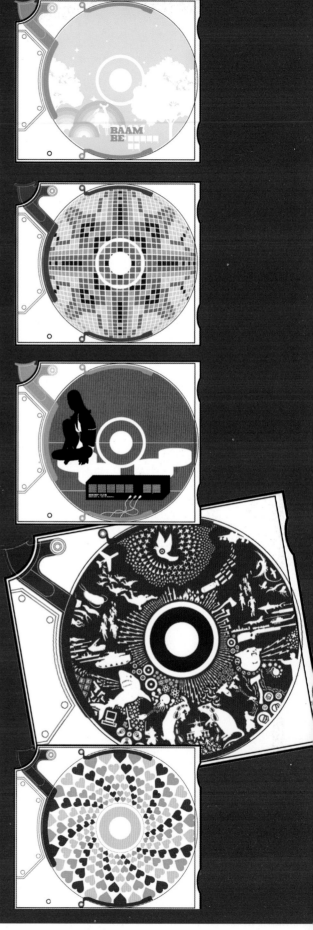

CLIENT
CARLOS SEGURA

DESIGN
CARLOS SEGURA

segura inc.

5INCH

There is a huge array of blank CDs on the market, but after seeing Carlos Segura's vast, eye-catching catalog of colorful designs for "5-inch" CDs, who would want to return to the unillustrated, plain alternative? Themes range from the abstract to the more figurative, with designs presented in color coordinated trigger cases, adding to the excitement and memorabilty of the user's experience. Overall, colors and designs are so strongly mnemonic that purchasers are bound to develop favorites, or even buy disks simply to establish a cherished collection of CD art.

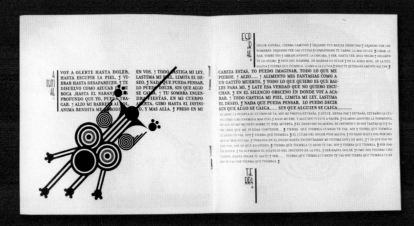

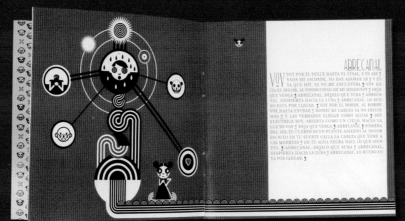

CLIENT
_____
LA BASE RECORDS

DESIGN
_____
LAURA VARSKY

ART DIRECTION
_____
LAURA VARSKY

COPYWRITING
_____
LAURA VARSKY

ILLUSTRATION
_____
CHRISTIAN MONTENEGRO

LAURA VARSKY DESIGN

BIENVENIDO, "NO DISCO"

In Laura Varsky's distinctive design, fluorescent pink ink combines with thick black and gray lines and circular motifs to create images that shout out to be remembered. Christian Montenegro's simple yet distinctive illustrations complement the vigorous colors to ensure that this design is unforgettable. Unusual typographic systems and groupings make up another factor that enhances and affirms the indelible nature of this impactful design.

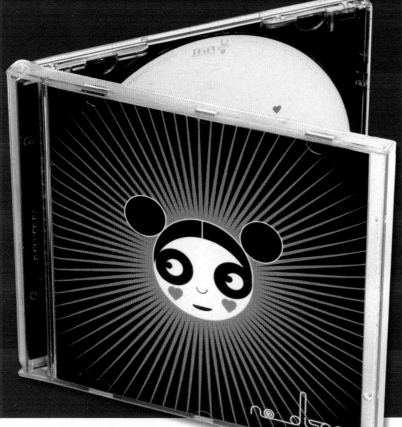

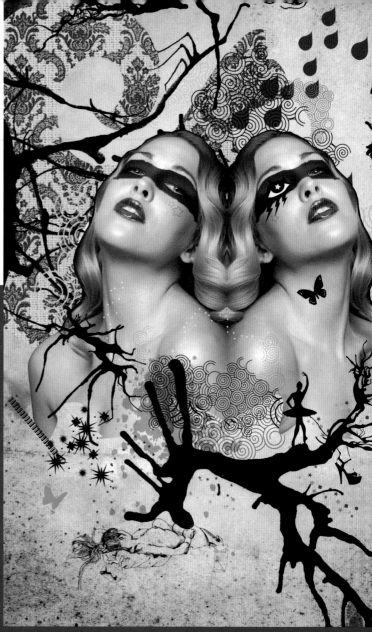

CLIENT
MINISTRY OF SOUND, LONDON

DESIGN
DAN MOORE AND LYDIA LAPINSKI

ART DIRECTION
STEVE PAYNE

ILLUSTRATION
STEVE PAYNE, DAN MOORE, AND LYDIA LAPINSKI

STUDIO OUTPUT

SECTION 8 THEATER

An eccentric illustrative style has been used by Studio Output to mimic the current fashion for burlesque, and to publicize theater nights at London nightclub Ministry of Sound. These images are memorable because they layer abstract splatter patterning over a mix of very unusual and unexpected figurative and nonfigurative imagery. The color combinations are also quite different, treating viewers to an exciting and distinctive visual feast, epitomizing the exaggerated theatrical events promised by Ministry of Sound.

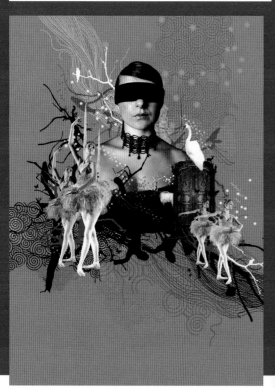

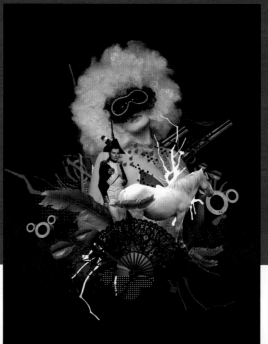

CLIENT
TAYLORS OF HARROGATE
DESIGN
JO ANDRADE AND PAUL PHILIPS
ART DIRECTION
JO ANDRADE
COPYWRITING
JO ANDRADE

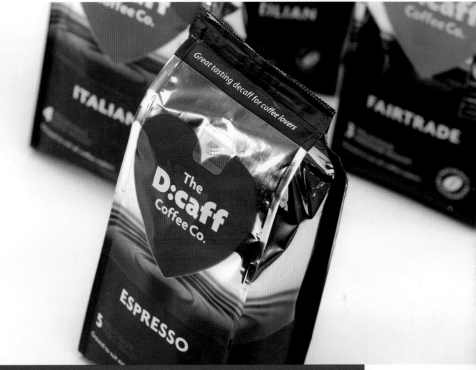

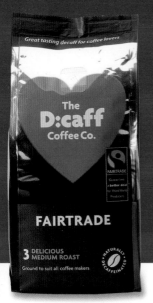

TAYLORS OF HARROGATE

THE D:CAFF COFFEE CO.

Within the vast array of goods on the shelves
of supermarkets, products need to have a strong
visual presence in order to be noticed and instantly
recognized. The D:caff Coffee Co. packaging employs a
number of eye-catching design techniques that ensure
notability together with easy recollection for repeat
purchasing. The hugely familiar and popular heart
shape, in bright colors, forms the anchor of each
pack. The contrasting mirror finish and matt
surfaces, plus a snappy namestyle, complete
this memorable visual synergy.

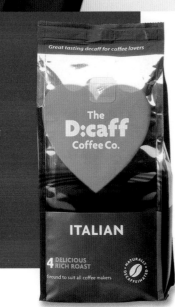

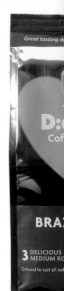

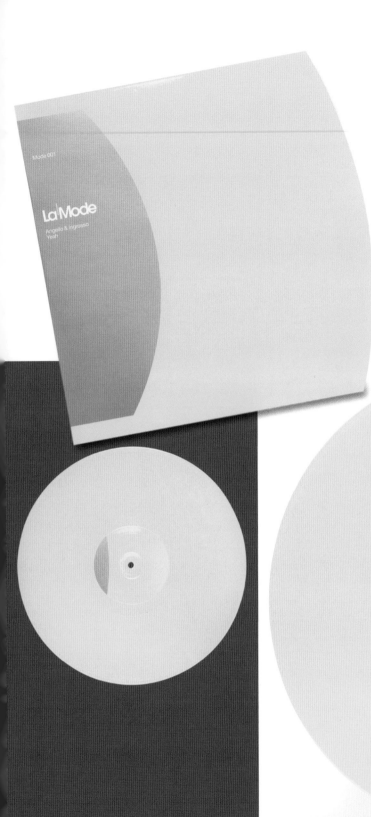

zion graphics

LA MODE

Bright yellow teamed with gray is an unusual color combination for La Mode records, and really stays in the mind's eye. Ricky Tillblad of Zion Graphics not only makes striking use of these two contrasting colors, but also mnemonic use of the circular shape of the yellow vinyl record, taking the curve of its edge as the inspiration for the sleeve design and record labeling. One of the most significant aspects of a very memorable design is the way in which the gray label appears to thread through the vinyl, showing the majority on the A-side and a slither on the B-side. The integration of vinyl color and the printed color of the sleeve makes for an eye-catching design that is likely to be collected for its looks as much as its music.

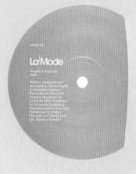

CLIENT
LA MODE RECORDS

DESIGN
RICKY TILLBLAD

ART DIRECTION
RICKY TILLBLAD

TYPOGRAPHY
RICKY TILLBLAD

CLIENT
_____
YOSHO

DESIGN
_____
CARLOS SEGURA

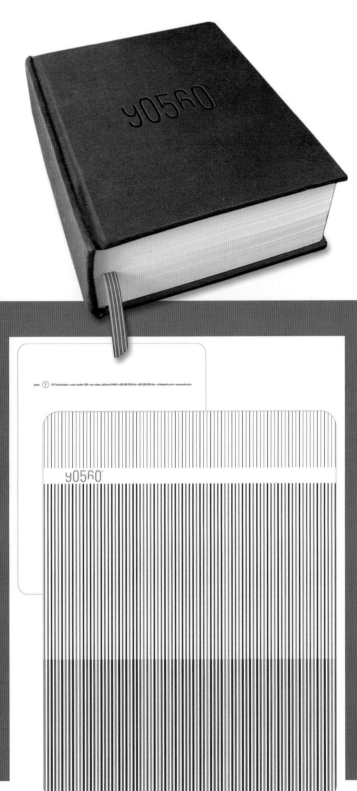

segura inc.

YOSHO IDENTITY

Distinctive use of color is the first reason that Carlos Segura's identity design for Yosho sticks in the mind. The second is the extensive use of closely spaced, finely colored stripes, which almost trick the eye into seeing a visual hum. The third and final reason that this identity is so mnemonic is Segura's clever use of numerals to substitute for the letterforms of the namestyle.

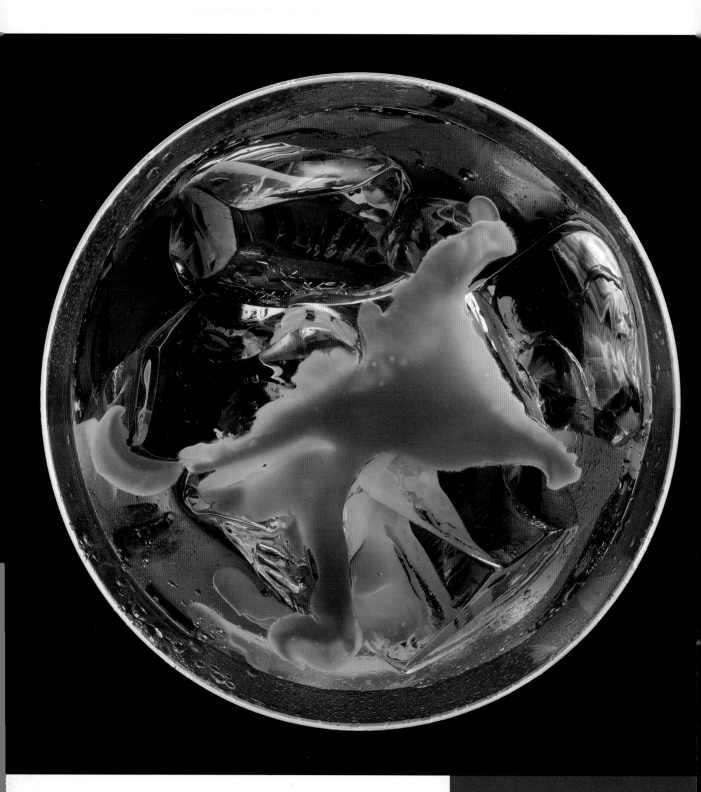

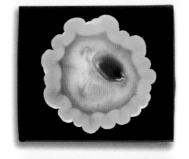

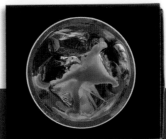

CLIENT
OQO/MARK CHAN

DESIGN
JAMIE ROBERTS

ART DIRECTION
JOHN SIMPSON

PHOTOGRAPHY
JOHN ROSS

SEA DESIGN

OQO BRAND IDENTITY

The name and namestyle for this Chinese restaurant was chosen for its palindromic qualities and lack of linguistic meaning. This enabled John Simpson and Jamie Roberts to use the repetitive circular shapes of the letterforms in a variety of visually powerful modes that dominate the environment in a very notable and identifiable manner. Bright, fresh colors contrast with black backgrounds and significantly add to the impact of this comprehensive branding.

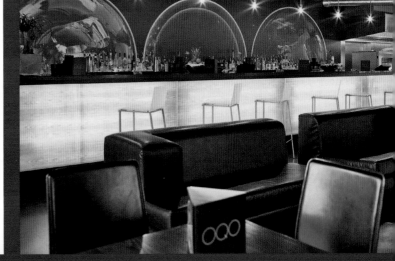

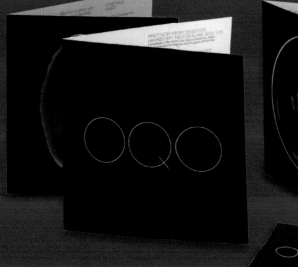

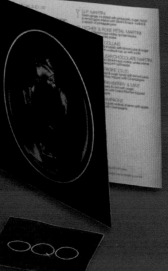

wuffdesign

IAN POOLEY, "SOUVENIRS"

Wuffdesign has used a brightly colored contemporary illustrative style to capture and hold the viewers' attention on the "Souvenirs" CD and album covers for Ian Pooley. Overlapping silhouettes mingle with sections of op art-inspired patterning, "creating a memorable visual narrative, where there is always something new to discover," comments Wuffdesign's Dani Muno.

Ian Pooley
Samo Iluzija

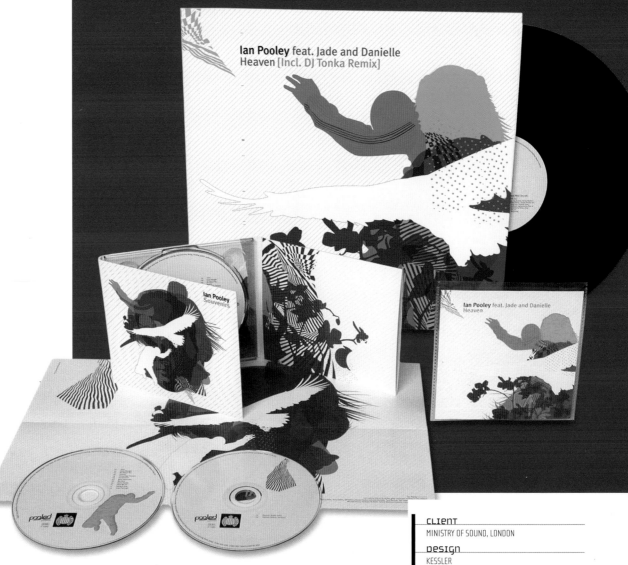

Ian Pooley feat. Jade and Danielle
Heaven [Incl. DJ Tonka Remix]

Ian Pooley
Souvenirs

Ian Pooley feat. Jade and Danielle
Heaven

CLIENT
MINISTRY OF SOUND, LONDON

DESIGN
KESSLER

ART DIRECTION
WUFFDESIGN

CLIENT
MINISTRY OF SOUND, LONDON

DESIGN
DAN MOORE AND LYDIA LAPINSKI

ART DIRECTION
DAN MOORE

COPYWRITING
STEVE WILSON-BEALES

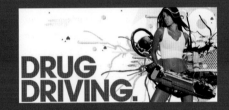

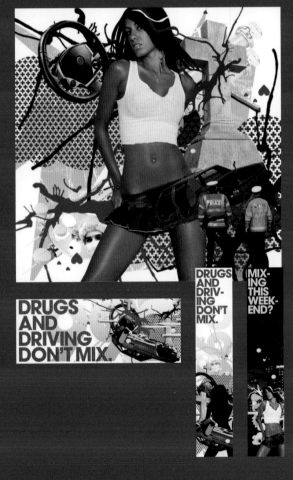

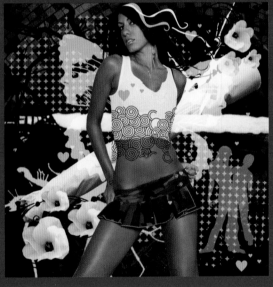

STUDIO OUTPUT

DRUGS AND DRIVING DON'T MIX

For the London nightclub Ministry of Sound's micro site, informing clubbers of the dangers of mixing drugs with driving, Dan Moore and Lydia Lapinski of Studio Output have developed very simple before-and-after animations. Utilizing two limited yet distinctive color palettes of contrasting tones and hues, cut-out imagery is layered in a contemporary and eye-catching way. It is not until the viewer's second glance that these memorable, trend-setting images start to reveal their darker message.

CLIENT
CLEAR MAGAZINE

DESIGN
KKIO HARDIN

ART DIRECTION
EMIN KADI

TYPOGRAPHY
KKIO HARDIN

ILLUSTRATION
KKIO HARDIN

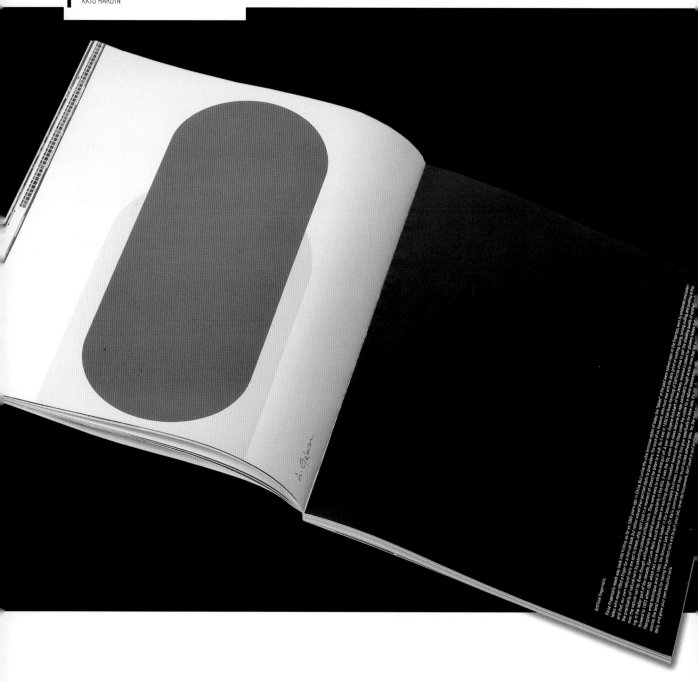

clear magazine

CLEAR MAGAZINE

These internal pages from volume IV issue 3 of *Clear* Magazine make dynamic and memorable use of color, as well as image and composition. The double-page spreads are dominated by bright, simple, large-scale illustrations by Kkio Hardin. These contrast so dramatically with the plain backgrounds that they leave a powerful and lasting impression in the mind's eye. Viewers are conditioned to expect magazine spreads to contain various levels of text and image, and the surprise of seeing these pages without any of these anticipated conventions adds to their memorable qualities.

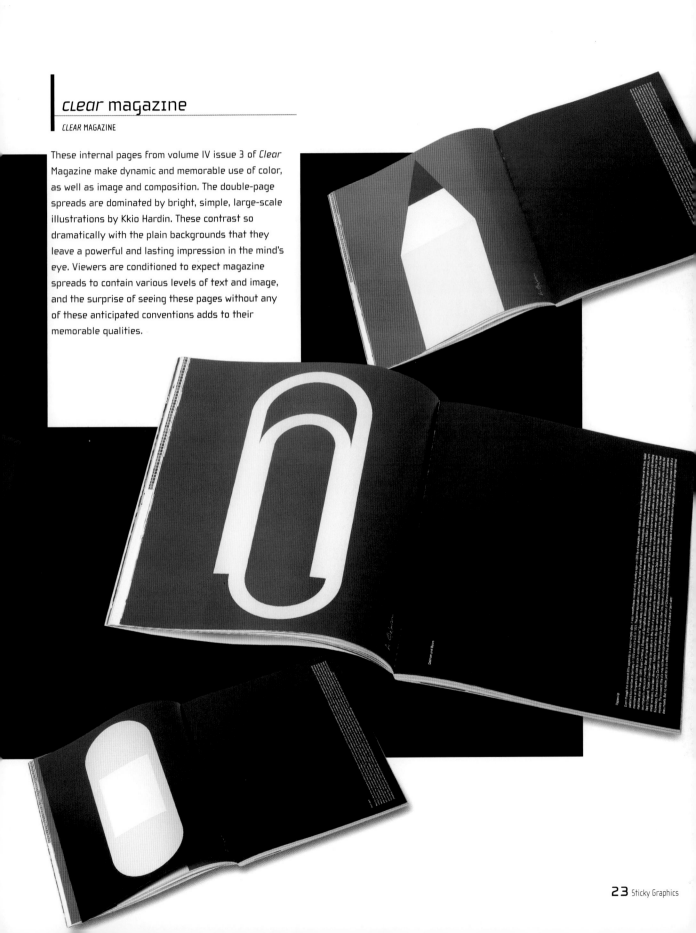

ODED EZER TYPOGRAPHY

THE ROOMS POSTER

In his poster for The Rooms project, Oded Ezer has created unforgettable 3-D black silicon letterforms. "I hope to create live, almost cinematic situations, where the letters act as characters that each have a role," explains Oded. The characters are memorable for their intrinsic visual qualities, rather than for any meaning that can be deduced from the Hebrew; the viewer is left with a haunting memory of these plump letterforms interacting in a disturbing manner with each other, and potentially outside of the frame of the poster.

CLIENT	
SELF-PROMOTIONAL	
DESIGN	
ODED EZER	
ART DIRECTION	
ODED EZER	
TYPOGRAPHY	
ODED EZER	
ILLUSTRATION	
ODED EZER	
PHOTOGRAPHY	
IDAN GIL	

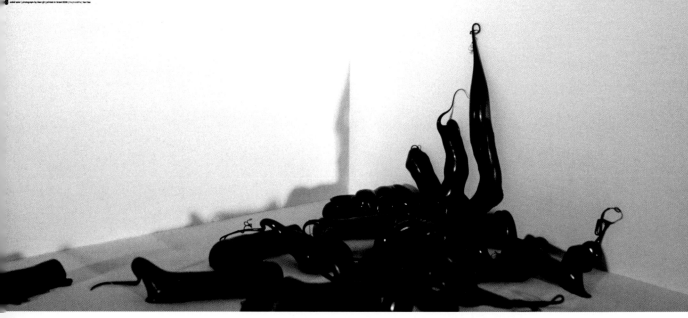

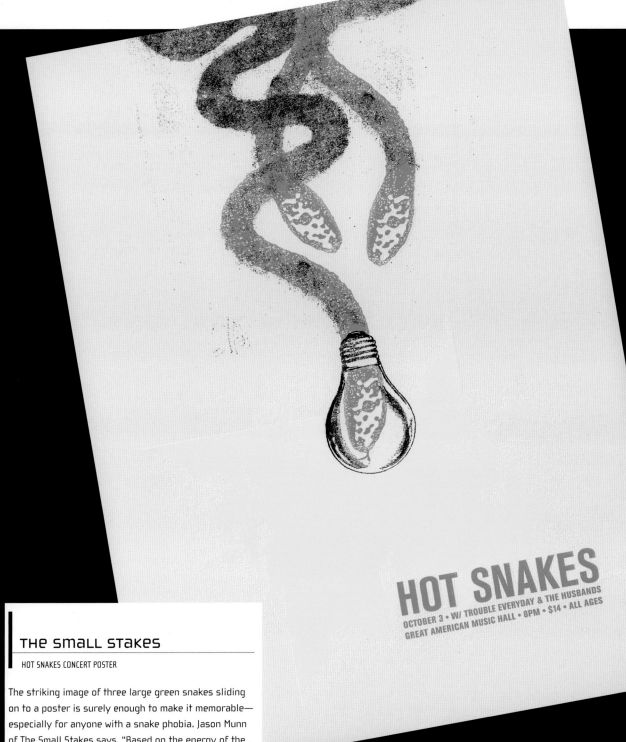

HOT SNAKES
OCTOBER 3 • W/ TROUBLE EVERYDAY & THE HUSBANDS
GREAT AMERICAN MUSIC HALL • 8PM • $14 • ALL AGES

THE SMALL STAKES

HOT SNAKES CONCERT POSTER

The striking image of three large green snakes sliding
on to a poster is surely enough to make it memorable—
especially for anyone with a snake phobia. Jason Munn
of The Small Stakes says, "Based on the energy of the
Hot Snakes' live show, I liked the idea of a snake entering
a light bulb and illuminating it." It's interesting that when
a concept is intriguing, and doesn't quite make sense,
it is inclined to be remembered, with a view to a solution
transpiring eventually.

CLIENT
HOT SNAKES
DESIGN
JASON MUNN

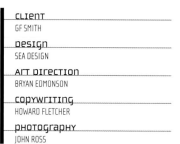

CLIENT
GF SMITH

DESIGN
SEA DESIGN

ART DIRECTION
BRYAN EDMONSON

COPYWRITING
HOWARD FLETCHER

PHOTOGRAPHY
JOHN ROSS

SEA DESIGN

GF SMITH WHITE BOOK, GF SMITH SWATCH BOOK

Printing inks and quality white paper are made for each other, and in both the white book that showcases GF Smith's papers, and the more functional GF Smith swatch book, the two come together in a striking and unforgettable manner. Photographic images of strongly colored inks swirling through water are printed as dynamic, giant organic masses flowing across vast white spaces with very little text. They attract attention because they contrast with the white stock, and also because they do not immediately appear as abstract; viewers want to form recognizable shapes out of the ink patterns. As this has the result of prolonging the viewing experience, it makes the designs very memorable.

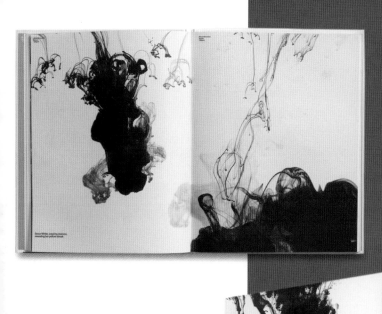

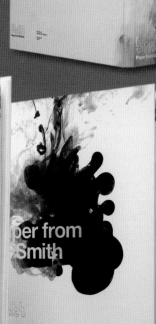

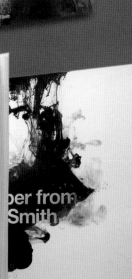

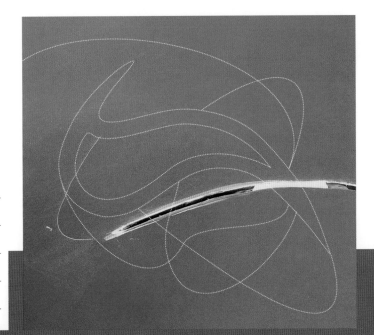

CLIENT
UNIVERSAL MUSIC

DESIGN
DIRK RUDOLPH

ART DIRECTION
DIRK RUDOLPH

TYPOGRAPHY
DIRK RUDOLPH

PHOTOGRAPHY
CHRISTOF SCHULTE

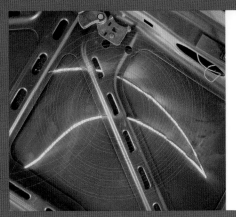

SONO BLAME

Florian Sikorski (Producer) | Martin Weiland (Songwriter, Producer) | Lennart A. Salomon (Singer)

Gleich mit ihrer Debütsingle „Keep Control" konnte das Hamburger Trio Sono einen Überraschungshit landen. Der smoothe Tech-House Track hebt sich angenehm aus der Masse der unzähligen Dance-Tracks hervor und eroberte - neben einer Platzierung in den UK Single Verkaufscharts - für sechs Wochen auch den Thron in den amerikanischen Billboard Dance Charts. In Deutschland hat sich „Keep Control" ebenfalls zu einem echten Club-Favourite entwickelt und konnte die Media Control Verkaufscharts auf Platz #31 entern. Wer also steckt hinter Sono? Zum einen Florian Sikorski, der einen Teil des Produzenten-Duos bildet. Von Kindesbeinen an mit der Musikwelt verbunden, genoss er zunächst eine klassische Musikausbildung, bevor ihn der damalige Hamburger Techno-Kultclub UNIT im Alter von 16 Jahren mit Clubmusik in Kontakt brachte. Er entschloss sich, fortan voll in die elektronische Musik einzutauchen. Mittlerweile kann er einen beträchtlichen Erfahrungsschatz als Tontechniker, Produzent und DJ aufweisen. So wurden seine Fertigkeiten als Tontechniker bereits von Weltstars wie den Backstreet Boys, *NSYNC und Britney Spears in Anspruch genommen. 1996 kreuzten sich dann die Wege von Florian und Martin Weiland, der seit seinem 15. Lebensjahr als DJ in angesagten Hamburger Clubs wie dem „Palladium", „Astoria", „Schlachthof" oder „Phonodrome" aufgelegt hat. Zurzeit präsentiert Martin regelmäßig seine „New Technique" im Kontor Club. Zusammen produzierten Florian und Martin verschiedene Remixe, u.a. für House-Queen Adeva, und bilden seit 2000 das Produzenten-Team von Sono. Fehlte also nur noch eine geeignete Stimme. Die fanden sie in Lennart A. Salomon, der seine Ursprünge in der Jazz und Funk Musik hat und auf eine Bühnenerfahrung sich die Liste der Künstler, die ihre Tracks kann. Mit dem Erfolg von „Keep Control" erweiterte sich die Liste der Künstler, die ihre Tracks von Sono neu aufmischen ließen, um so illustre Namen wie u.a. Tom Novy, Schiller, The Ones oder Rudolfkeup by Florian Sikorski/Lennart Salomon/Martin Weiland | Published by Hazelwood Music Prod. GmbH/Loop Associated Publisher Warner Chappell Music GmbH/ Smarten-up Musikverlag/Universal Music Publishing | Produced by Florian Sikorski/Lennart Salomon/Martin Weiland | Design by www.dirkrudolph.de |

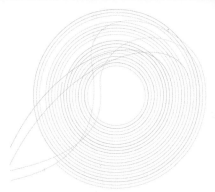

DIRK RUDOLPH

SONO, "BLAME"

Who can forget a scratch to their car—its shape, its depth, and when it happened? The cover design for "Blame" memorably uses images of scratched car body panels to great effect. Incisions have been created that follow the path of the Sono mark, and shots have been overlaid by more complex, graphic representations of scratches, using spirals of orange and magenta dotted lines. Typographic styling of the titling also reflects and corresponds with the weight and design approach of the scratchy mark-making.

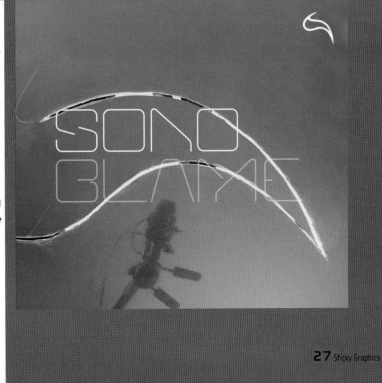

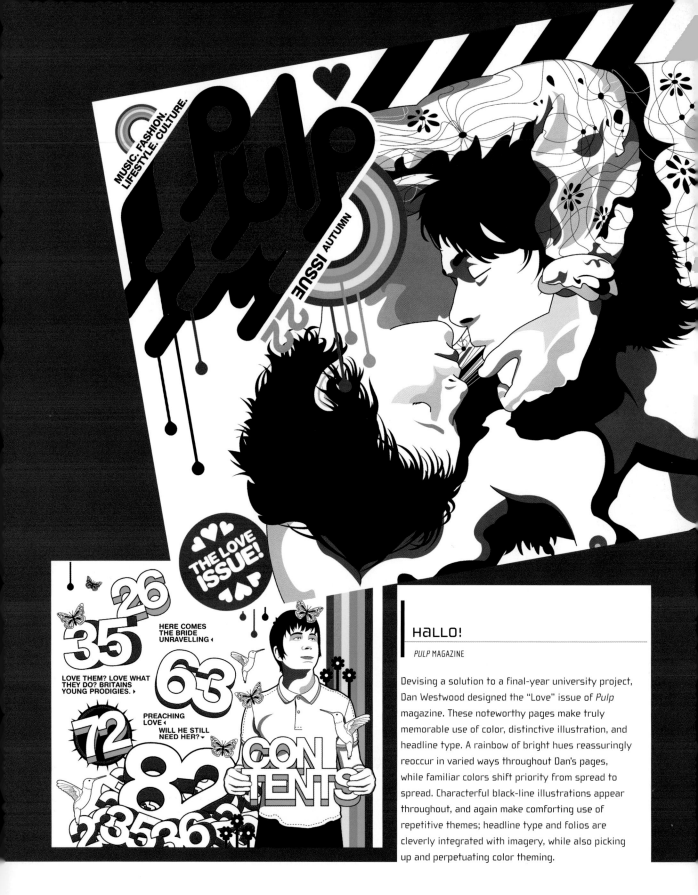

MUSIC. FASHION.
LIFESTYLE. CULTURE.

Pulp

ISSUE AUTUMN

22

THE LOVE
ISSUE!

35 26

HERE COMES
THE BRIDE
UNRAVELLING ‹

LOVE THEM? LOVE WHAT
THEY DO? BRITAINS
YOUNG PRODIGIES. ‹

63

72

PREACHING
LOVE ‹
WILL HE STILL
NEED HER? ‹

82

CON
TENTS

23526

HALLO!

PULP MAGAZINE

Devising a solution to a final-year university project, Dan Westwood designed the "Love" issue of *Pulp* magazine. These noteworthy pages make truly memorable use of color, distinctive illustration, and headline type. A rainbow of bright hues reassuringly reoccur in varied ways throughout Dan's pages, while familiar colors shift priority from spread to spread. Characterful black-line illustrations appear throughout, and again make comforting use of repetitive themes; headline type and folios are cleverly integrated with imagery, while also picking up and perpetuating color theming.

Click, clack, whirr. Click, clack, whirr Rachael Matthews is working on her French knitting machine. She doesn't stop to speak to me, she keeps winding away. "We haven't got long," she says. "The invitations have already gone out." And indeed, in two months' time, the first ever completely knitted wedding is taking place.

The confetti will be knitted. The cake will be knitted. The dress will be purl. The flowers plain. Cast on, knit one for the camera. This is every girl's dream. A proper woollen wedding.

Rachael Matthews (click clack whirr) is making blue bunting. A young woman dressed in an artfully frumpy fashion, she is standing in the Pump House Gallery, London, surrounded by balls of blue wool and a few helpers, who are knitting contentedly. Rachael, the chair

of "Cast Off", the Knitting Club For Boys and Girls, has sent wedding patterns to knitting groups nationwide.

Kettering will make the candles. Wells is working on the ham sandwiches.

The North Circular Knitters will do the doves (don't ask). "And people will just make whatever they want. Someone's sending a bouquet of booties in Dutch colours." The artist Mary Gee might contribute one of her trademark knitted vaginas, I say. Rachael is delighted. "That's the thing about weddings, isn't it" she says. "You never know what people are going to give you."

Indeed. An art student I meet in the gallery is weighing up his options. He sighs gently and

folds his arms (his shirt has a pattern of teddy-bears). "I think I'll knit them a PlayStation. Or maybe a life-size chimney sweep, for luck."

Everyone who contributes is invited to the ceremony. "You may knit through the reception," reads the invite. "There will be drinks but you may want to bring a picnic, as the food is knitted."

But under all the yarn and fluff, there is a real commitment-taking place. Freddie Robbins, an artist working primarily in the medium of wool (her gloves for severed thumbs were on display in the V&A last year) is marrying metal artist Ben Coode Adams. They are the perfect couple for a knitted wedding. The only

couple, perhaps. I find the bride downstairs, handing out flyers for her nuptials "My parents think it's a bit weird, that my wedding should be a spoof of wedding culture," she says. But then, in some ways, the enterprise makes sense. As Rachael says: "There's a lot of time and care invested in hand knitting. Basically, a lot of love."

Hermione Eyre

"THE CONFETTI WILL BE KNITTED... THE CAKE WILL BE KNITTED... A PROPER WOOLEN WEDDING"

HERE COMES THE bride

UN RAVELLING **35**

HERE COMES THE bride UN RAVELLING 36

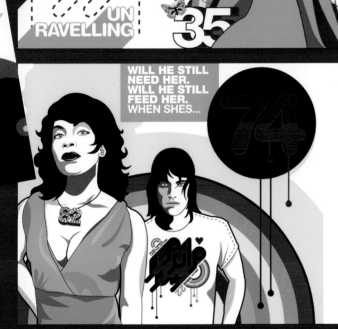

WILL HE STILL NEED HER. WILL HE STILL FEED HER. WHEN SHES...

74

PULP WILL SHE STILL NEED HIM?

A quarter of UK brides are older than the groom. Elizabeth Heathcote on why this season's must have is a younger man.

Sheryl Crow's announcement earlier this month that she is going to marry a man nine years her junior – the cycling legend Lance Armstrong, 34 – barely caused a stir. It has become so de rigueur for stars to settle down with men a decade or two younger than themselves that the celebrity press can barely rouse itself to trot out a toy-boy jibe. At 42, Demi Moore is 15 years older than her lover Ashton Kutcher. Judy Finnigan is eight years ahead of her 49-year-old husband. Madonna, Emma Thompson, Susan Sarandon, Cameron Diaz, Whitney Houston, Charlotte Rampling and Joely Richardson are all men at least five years younger than themselves. Barbara Hershey's lover of seven years, the British actor Naveen Andrews, is 21 years her junior.

And where thespians lead... A new study by Dr Maire Ni Bhrolchain of Southampton University and published by the Office for National Statistics shows that in a quarter of British marriages, the bride is now older than the groom. In one in 10 she is at least five years older, and this proportion has doubled in 20 years. You can write off a celebrity's penchant for a pliable younger buck as the logical extension of the control freakery that got her name in lights in the first place, but something bigger is clearly going on

There are ominous contributing factors. Women look, act and dress younger for longer. Many are no longer hunting for a (typically older) breadwinner. There are more second marriages, and the age difference is most pronounced where the woman has been divorced previously. Plus women are having children (and

therefore often looking for a mate) later, and as any single woman over 35 will tell you, men in their late 30s and 40s have usually had their children already or don't want any.

Adrienne Burgess, a relationship researcher, believes this last point in particular has persuaded women to widen the net. "My feeling is that men have always been prepared to look at older women," she says. "It was women who used to say, 'I can't go out with him, he's a child.' Plus women were looking for financial security, but that's no longer the case."

Sally Rogers, a 39-year-old teacher in London, was "surprised" when she found herself with Adam, 31, her partner of three years and the man she hopes to marry. "I did expect to go out with someone older — someone sorted, with their own house and so on," she says.

Does she resent the fact that he's still renting and earns less than she does? "Who stays with someone because of material things? Women have their own lives, jobs, money, houses," she says. "All they want men to give is themselves. I had been looking for long enough when I met Adam to appreciate how brilliant he is."

Janet Reibstein, a psychologist and teacher at Exeter University, believes that women having children later has eroded the taboo for men, too. "It is the fundamental change," she says. "By having children later, women have stretched the image of the 'sexual woman' into what used to be the 'older woman'. That makes it more permissible for a man to be with her – if she's seen as

sexy, desirable and powerful, then so is the man who is with her. "I call this the Mick effect; four years ago I discussed older women with my friend, Mick, who made it clear that they are very sexy when a man is in his early 20s, pretty sexy when he turns 30, but sorry, from 40 on he is only going to fancy younger women. But when I ask him again (now aged 45), he musters the courage to admit that he does fancy women in their 50s.

"There is basically a war going on inside a chap's head," he says, "between identity and instinct. The truth is that you think two or three times before you let yourself fancy a woman who is older - it's about how it reflects on you." In other words, if Ashton Kutcher and Justin Timberlake can do it, he can own up too.

Both sexes are clear about the positives. "Adam has no catalogue of failed relationships, no children," says Sally. "He's a physically strapping man with no sign of decay. And he doesn't have erectile dysfunction, which was an issue with some of the men in their 40s when I dated. It's fun - he has all his life ahead of him, and he's excited by it. And I do think sometimes, hopefully this way I won't be left a widow." The appeal of the older woman, says Mick, is that she is powerful, sexy and financially independent, which can look particularly attractive to a generation of young men in search of more equal relationships.

"The overwhelming evidence is that men in their 20s want to share the burden of breadwinning," says Ms Burgess. "In fact, younger couples where the woman doesn't contribute financially are the least likely to last." Maybe what stands out in these relationships is a strange equality. "Men still have more social power," says Ms Burgess. "If she earns more and is a bit more worldly,

" A QUARTER OF UK BRIDES ARE OLDER THAN THE GROOM"

As a nation we're prone to dismiss our children's success (the teams were too small) and delight in hounding those guilty of youthful folly (see Wayne Rooney). As to counterbalance this, we have produced this relativity none of some of our extraordinary young talent. Descendants to authors, actors to chefs, they are all 16 or under. Welcome to the future.

LOVE THEM? LOVE WHAT THEY DO?

britajns YOUNG PRODIGIES

63

Fraser Doherty 16
Entrepreneur

David Howell 16
Chess Genius

Victoria Willis 16
Chef

Claudia Merikula 15
Model

64

PULP BRITAIN'S YOUNG PRODIGIES

CLIENT
SELF-PROMOTIONAL

DESIGN
DAN WESTWOOD

ART DIRECTION
DAN WESTWOOD

TYPOGRAPHY
DAN WESTWOOD

ILLUSTRATION
DAN WESTWOOD

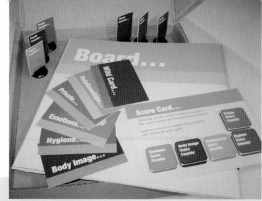

Turbulence...

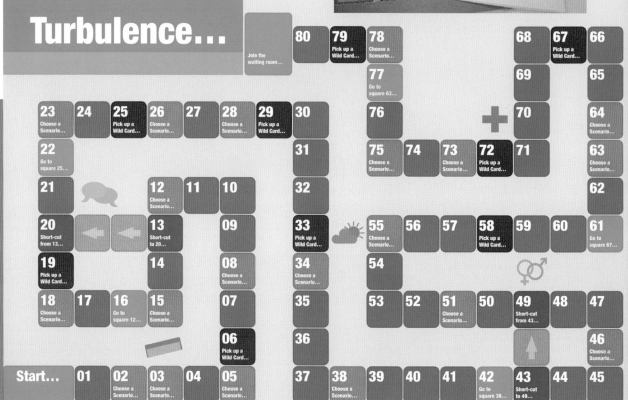

Join the waiting room...

| 80 | 79 Pick up a Wild Card... | 78 Choose a Scenario... | | | 68 | 67 Pick up a Wild Card... | 66 |

77 Go to square 63...

23 Choose a Scenario... | 24 | 25 Pick up a Wild Card... | 26 Choose a Scenario... | 27 | 28 Choose a Scenario... | 29 Pick up a Wild Card... | 30

22 Go to square 25...

21

20 Short-cut from 13...

19 Pick up a Wild Card...

18 Choose a Scenario... | 17 | 16 Go to square 12... | 15 Choose a Scenario...

12 Choose a Scenario... | 11 | 10

13 Short-cut to 20...

14

09

08 Choose a Scenario...

07

06 Pick up a Wild Card...

Start... | 01 | 02 Choose a Scenario... | 03 Choose a Scenario... | 04 | 05 Choose a Scenario...

31
32
33 Pick up a Wild Card...
34 Choose a Scenario...
35
36
37 | 38 Choose a Scenario... | 39 | 40 | 41 | 42 Go to square 38... | 43 Short-cut to 49... | 44 | 45

76
75 Choose a Scenario... | 74 | 73 Choose a Scenario... | 72 Pick up a Wild Card... | 71
70
69

55 Choose a Scenario... | 56 | 57 | 58 Pick up a Wild Card... | 59 | 60 | 61 Go to square 67...
54
53 | 52 | 51 Choose a Scenario... | 50 | 49 Short-cut from 43... | 48 | 47
46 Choose a Scenario...

64 Choose a Scenario...
63 Choose a Scenario...
62
65
66

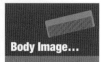
Body Image...

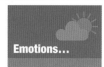
Emotions...

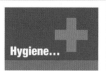
Hygiene...

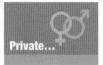
Private...

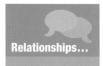
Relationships...

Wild Card...

TWELVE20

TURBULENCE BOARD GAME

This health-related board game is designed to appeal to, and be remembered by, teenagers. Bright colors have been used to attract young people, to help them remember key health issues and put recommendations into practice. The colors used are: pink for body image; cyan for emotions; dark blue for hygiene; orange for sexual health; and green for relationships. As a result of these carefully considered associations, healthcare advice becomes easy to remember and easy to search out when needed.

CLIENT
CANNOCK CHASE COUNCIL AND NHS
DESIGN
DARREN LANGHAM AND MATTHEW TULLETT
ART DIRECTION
DARREN LANGHAM AND MATTHEW TULLETT
COPYWRITING
DARREN LANGHAM AND LISA SHEPARD
ILLUSTRATION
DARREN LANGHAM

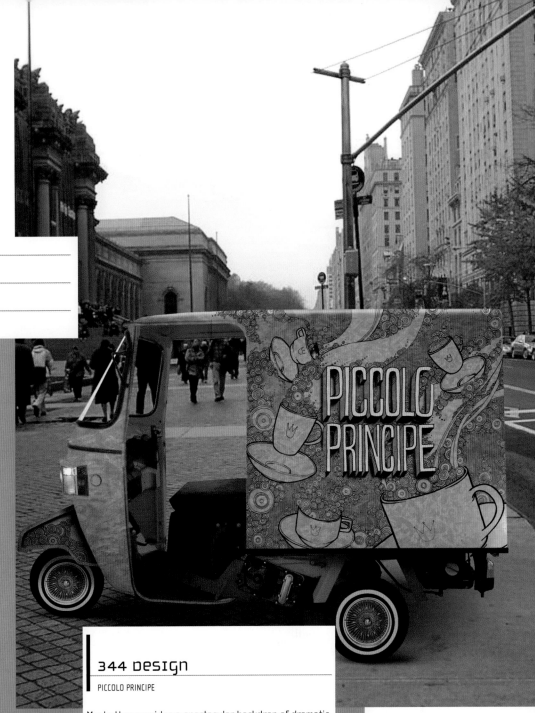

CLIENT
PRINCIPE AND COMPANY
DESIGN
STEFAN G. BUCHER
ILLUSTRATION
STEFAN G. BUCHER

344 DESIGN

PICCOLO PRINCIPE

Manhattan provides a spectacular backdrop of dramatic skyscrapers, crowds of people, colorful stores, and large cars. Everything is larger than life, and Piccolo Principe wanted to stand out and be remembered in this location. Stefan Bucher first selected a very unusual and comical small vehicle to be used as a vending truck in New York. Then he designed its surface to be painted in golds, including gold leaf, so it appeared bright, reflective, and eye-catching. As with many mnemonic designs, it is the unexpected combination of visual elements, including the vehicle itself, in relation to its surroundings, that makes this project significant.

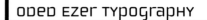

ODED EZER TYPOGRAPHY

BIOTYPOGRAPHY POSTER

Biotypography is the name given by Oded Ezer for "the medium of creating typographic mutations, by combining nature and typography." This memorable poster design displays a number of Hebrew letterforms that have taken on the character of insects. "I have treated myself as a typographic scientist, who can produce these creatures that have typographic information implanted into their DNA," Oded concludes. The poster is particularly memorable because these "typo-insects" appear giant-sized and seem surprisingly threatening as they approach the viewer.

CLIENT
SELF-PROMOTIONAL

DESIGN
ODED EZER

ART DIRECTION
ODED EZER

ILLUSTRATION
ODED EZER

PHOTOGRAPHY
IDAN GIL

TYPOGRAPHY
ODED EZER

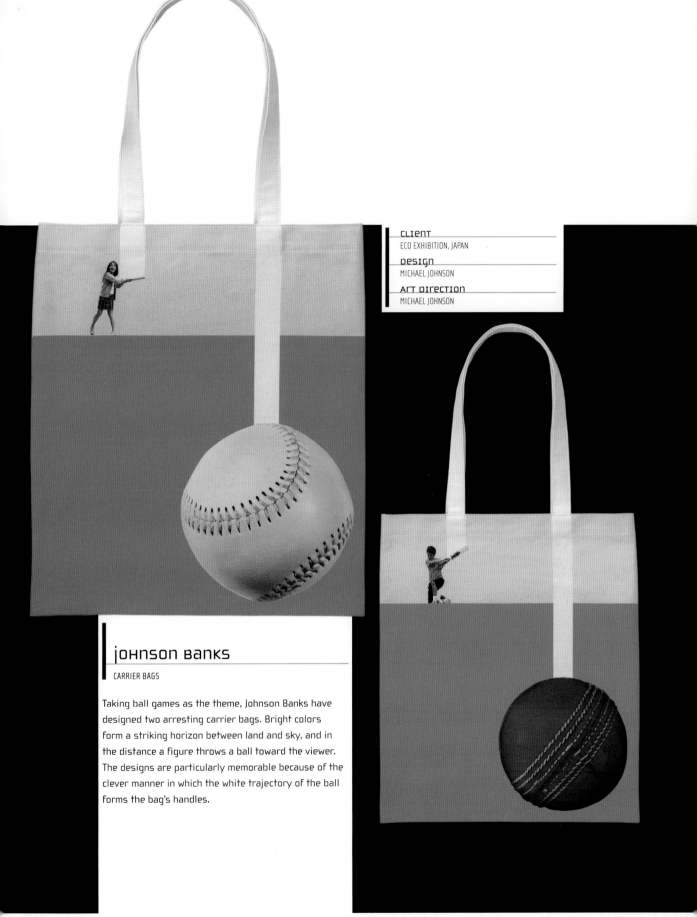

CLIENT

ECO EXHIBITION, JAPAN

DESIGN

MICHAEL JOHNSON

ART DIRECTION

MICHAEL JOHNSON

JOHNSON BANKS

CARRIER BAGS

Taking ball games as the theme, Johnson Banks have
designed two arresting carrier bags. Bright colors
form a striking horizon between land and sky, and in
the distance a figure throws a ball toward the viewer.
The designs are particularly memorable because of the
clever manner in which the white trajectory of the ball
forms the bag's handles.

rebecca foster design

CHELSEA COLLEGE OF ART AND DESIGN SUMMER SHOW INVITATIONS

These invitations by Rebecca Foster Design use strong color to represent a group of students undertaking a journey. They were mailed out separately with the intention of utilizing the color mnemonically, so the color in the second invitation builds on the memory of the color seen in the first one. An individual line symbolizes a student's progress along a creative path, and the increasingly dramatic forms and shapes in subsequent designs reflect the individuality of each course taken.

Aesun Kim

Mi Young Kim

James Maher

David McAllister

John Miers

Liz Murray

Sean O'Connor

Chiara Perini

Dai Roberts

Chris Rochelle

Rebecca Simmons

Carina Thoren

Haruto Toyoda

Lorcan Vallely

Michael Williams

Hannah Williamson

Craig Andrews

Samantha Archetti

Rachel Barbaresi

Pascale Berthier

Cecilia Bonilla-Jabif

Dana Brintz

Laura Cariola

Xiao Yan Cheng

Young Mi Chun

Marcus Cope

Charmi Gada

Sara Gates

Rui Inacio

Daniel Kennedy-Martin

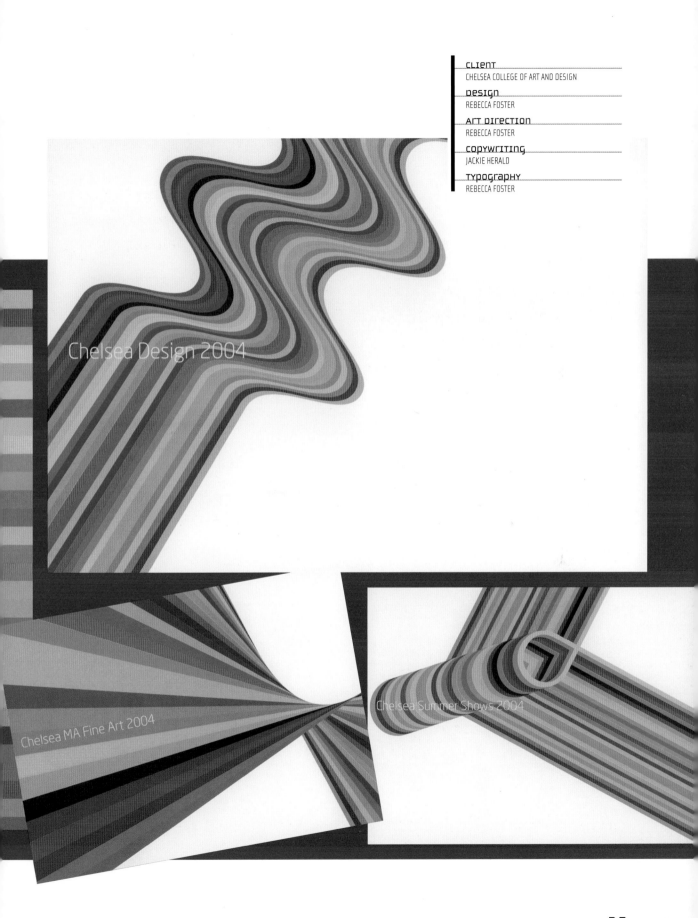

CLIENT
CHELSEA COLLEGE OF ART AND DESIGN

DESIGN
REBECCA FOSTER

ART DIRECTION
REBECCA FOSTER

COPYWRITING
JACKIE HERALD

TYPOGRAPHY
REBECCA FOSTER

Chelsea Design 2004

Chelsea MA Fine Art 2004

Chelsea Summer Shows 2004

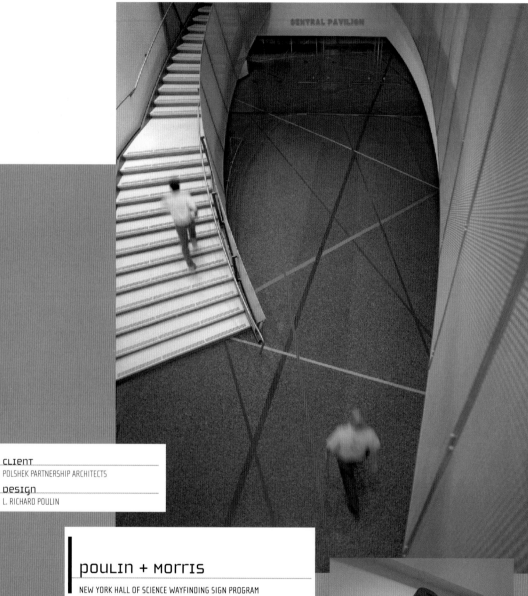

POULIN + MORRIS

NEW YORK HALL OF SCIENCE WAYFINDING SIGN PROGRAM

Poulin + Morris have utilized the memorable aspect
of strong, distinctive colors to produce this effective
wayfinding system for the New York Hall of Science.
Using primary hues, each area of this location is
associated with a thematic color. This allows visitors
and users of the building to simply search by color
for the destination they require. Adhered to the floor,
pathways of colored vinyl reinforce the color theming
and make tracks to final locations without the need for
extra language-based signage.

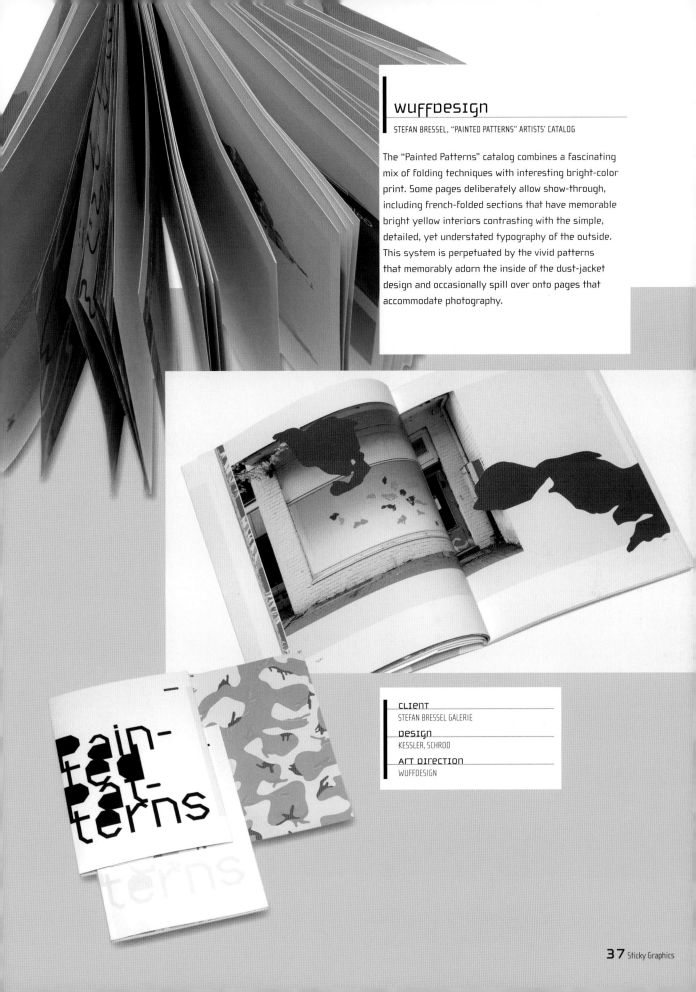

wuffdesign

STEFAN BRESSEL, "PAINTED PATTERNS" ARTISTS' CATALOG

The "Painted Patterns" catalog combines a fascinating mix of folding techniques with interesting bright-color print. Some pages deliberately allow show-through, including french-folded sections that have memorable bright yellow interiors contrasting with the simple, detailed, yet understated typography of the outside. This system is perpetuated by the vivid patterns that memorably adorn the inside of the dust-jacket design and occasionally spill over onto pages that accommodate photography.

CLIENT
STEFAN BRESSEL GALERIE

DESIGN
KESSLER, SCHROD

ART DIRECTION
WUFFDESIGN

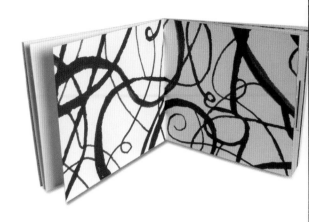

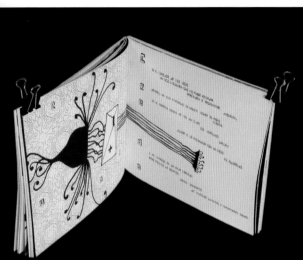

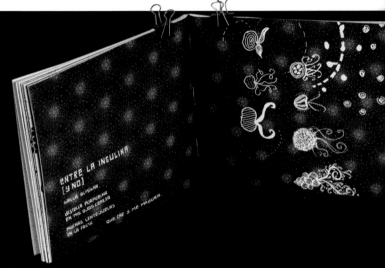

Laura Varsky Design

VERDESOLAR

The integration of illustration and typography have created a distinctive and memorable design for Verdesolar. Poetry merges and flows in and around imagery, forming one cohesive and fascinating whole. The format of this book is also memorable, with small, almost square pages providing the reader with an intimate journey.

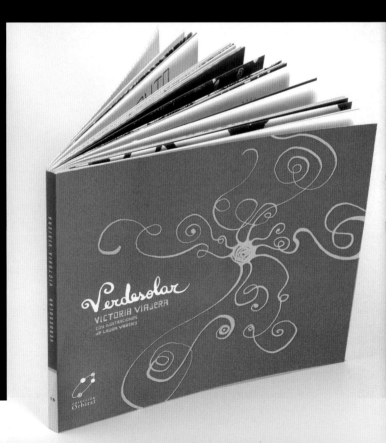

CLIENT
EDICIONES ORBITAL VICTORIA VIAJERA

DESIGN
LAURA VARSKY

ART DIRECTION
LAURA VARSKY

COPYWRITING
LAURA VARSKY

ILLUSTRATION
LAURA VARSKY

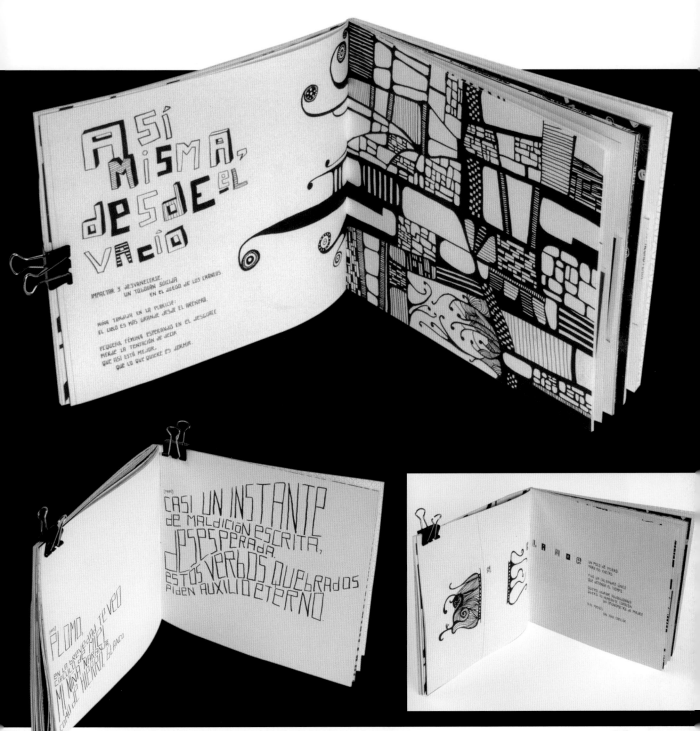

bankerwessel

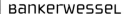

TOWN PLANS OF SWEDEN

Books on the subject of architecture are expected
to contain photographs and artist's impressions
of buildings, together with flatplans and scaled
drawings. *Town Plans of Sweden* depicts such different
interpretations of buildings and streets that it is very
distinctive and leaves a lasting impression on readers.
Fascinating aerial views of dark-brown 3-D models of
streets contrast and complement vibrant geometric
shapes grouped like blocks of houses, and the book
emits a sense of fun that is summed up in the word
"smile" on the back cover. Compositionally, the
monochrome aerial models use space and scale
in totally the opposite manner to the vibrant
geometric shapes; this also identifies the book
as unusual and memorable.

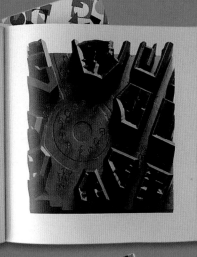

CLIENT
ARKITEKTURMUSEET

DESIGN
IDA WESSEL

ART DIRECTION
IDA WESSEL

ILLUSTRATION
JONAS BANKER

PHOTOGRAPHY
NIKLAS DAHLSKOL

TYPOGRAPHY
IDA WESSEL

pOULIN + MOrrIS

COMMUNI—CARDS 1 AND 2

Communi—Cards 1 and 2 have been designed by
L. Richard Poulin of Poulin + Morris to assist patients
at the Mount Sinai Medical Center to communicate.
He has designed a series of simple, memorable, iconic
images as a substitute for written language. They can
be pointed to, by patients or hospital staff, in situations
where intelligible speech is difficult. A haunting
androgynous figure is shown as the primary focus
of each square, and is often seen acting out ailments
and difficulties. Three simple changes are used to
differentiate between points relating to ailments
(orange), treatment (blue), and patient requests
(green), thus instantly and memorably connecting
with the urgency of the message.

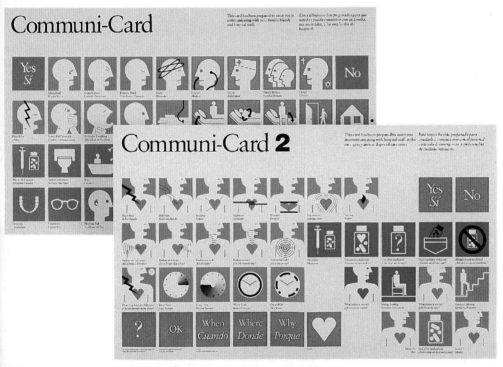

CLIENT
MOUNT SINAI MEDICAL CENTER
DESIGN
L. RICHARD POULIN

The Small Stakes

PEDRO THE LION

This poster for the band Pedro the Lion is memorable for a number of reasons, all of which are associated with designer Jason Munn's use of imagery and color. "Based on the biblical reference that the lamb and the lion will lay next to each other in heaven," says Jason, "this poster subtly acknowledges what really happens when these two animals get together." Jason's style of type, use of illustration, and choice of color are also memorable because they refer to the appealing genre of children's books, as well as using dynamic relationships of scale and space.

SUMMER TOUR 2004 W/ *john vanderslice*

CLIENT
PEDRO THE LION

DESIGN
JASON MUNN

ILLUSTRATION
JASON MUNN

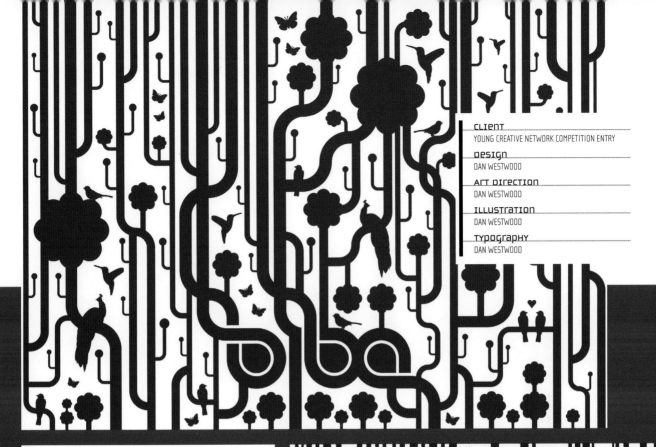

CLIENT
YOUNG CREATIVE NETWORK COMPETITION ENTRY

DESIGN
DAN WESTWOOD

ART DIRECTION
DAN WESTWOOD

ILLUSTRATION
DAN WESTWOOD

TYPOGRAPHY
DAN WESTWOOD

HALLO!

YOUNG CREATIVE NETWORK COMPETITION ENTRY

The use of dramatic, contrasting color is one of the most assured ways of attracting attention to a design. Overlapping and intertwining black linework forms the basis of Dan Westwood's solution for a redesign of iconic 1960s brand, Biba. This intricate network of interconnecting black lines is as intriguing and evocative as electronic circuitry. As a result of brave and highly contrasting use of black against bright white, this design creates a dramatic lasting impression. Each black and white grid, on first viewing, seems to be the same. However, after more detailed inspection, small, seasonally inspired silhouettes become visible, adding to the design's memorability, and enabling subtle differentiation between the styles of spring, summer, fall, and winter.

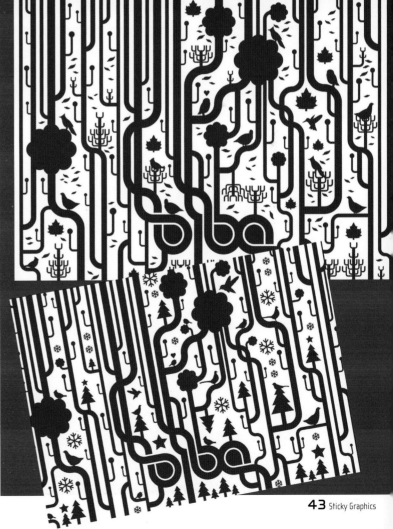

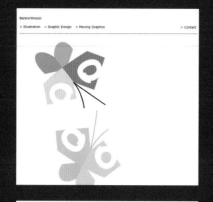

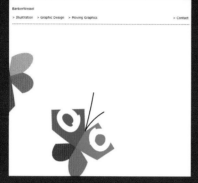

CLIENT
BANKERWESSEL

DESIGN
IDA WESSEL

ART DIRECTION
JONAS BANKER

ILLUSTRATION
JONAS BANKER

TYPOGRAPHY
IDA WESSEL

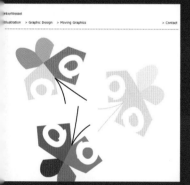

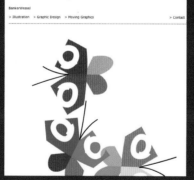

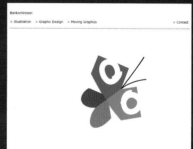

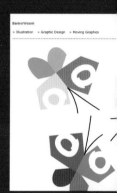

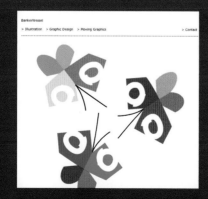

BANKERWESSEL

INTRODUCTORY SEQUENCE FOR BANKERWESSEL HOMEPAGE

Brightly colored animated graphic butterflies fly across the screen on the homepage of the BankerWessel Web site. Their iconic simplicity verges on a childlike quality that is not only memorable for its vibrancy and vitality, but also for the fun and humor that gives the creatures personalities. Visitors to the site are bound to be captivated, and will remember it as "the one with the butterflies," suggesting to colleagues that they should take a look too.

form fünf Bremen

WERNER SCHEFFER CORPORATE DESIGN

The extremely unusual use of typography within this identity for Werner Scheffer makes it distinctive and notable. Unexpected incremental increases and decreases in letterspacing, together with very brave compositional groupings and alignments, form the kind of design surprises that are remembered. The *pièce de resistance*, however, is the word "sport." This is printed on the letter-heading and shows through the window envelope in a position that makes it precisely line up with the word "journalist" on the envelope itself.

WERNER SCHEF F ER
S P ORTJOURNALIST

REDAKTION@SCHEFSPORT.DE
WWW.SCHEFSPORT.DE
FON 04431.1268
MOBIL 0172.4246385
FAX 04431.709223
KIEBITZWEG 3A
27793 WILDESHAUSEN

VOLKSBANK WILDESHAUSER GEEST
BLZ. 28066214
KONTONR. 13822300

> Contact

KIEBITZWEG 3A
27793 WILDESHAUSEN
WERNER SCHEF F ER

S P OR T J OURNALIST

mnemonics
Bright Pink

Lapley Studio, Lapley
ST199JS Staffordshire
England

CLIENT
WERNER SCHEFFER
DESIGN
WIEBKE BECKER
ART DIRECTION
DANIEL BASTIAN

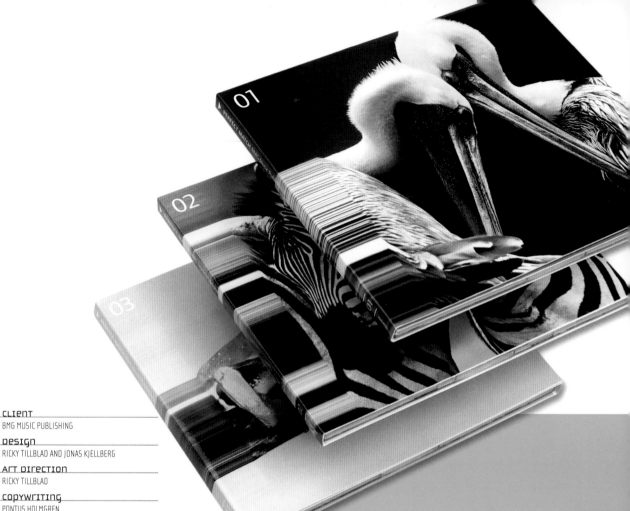

CLIENT
BMG MUSIC PUBLISHING

DESIGN
RICKY TILLBLAD AND JONAS KJELLBERG

ART DIRECTION
RICKY TILLBLAD

COPYWRITING
PONTUS HOLMGREN

TYPOGRAPHY
RICKY TILLBLAD AND JONAS KJELLBERG

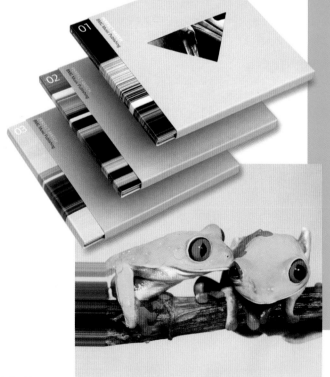

ZION GRAPHICS

"PERFECT MATCH"

This three-volume set of CD packaging for BMG Music Publishing utilizes shots of exotic wildlife, which bring memorable color combinations to these covers. Zion Graphics have stretched the left edge of each image to create colorful contrasting stripes that run round on to the back of the packs, and are revealed as they extend beyond the edge of the shortened slipcases. This clever use of wildlife photography, Photoshop, and attractive die-cut slipcases has created a strong mnemonic that guarantees the viewer will not only remember this design, but will also want to purchase not just one but all three CDs in this set.

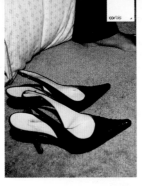
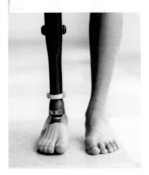
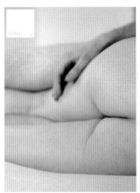
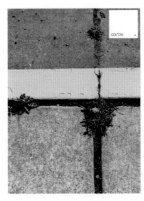

CLIENT	
CORBIS	
DESIGN	
CARLOS SEGURA	

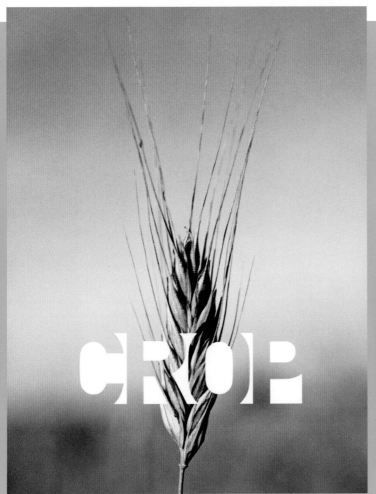

segura inc.

CROP

Segura Inc. makes particularly memorable use of cropping in its designs for Corbis photo library. It takes a single-minded approach to the manner in which selected shots are presented, showing one main mnemonic image on each page. This particular series of catalogs is entitled "Crop" and has an impactful typographic namestyle that also echoes Segura's close-cropped treatment of imagery.

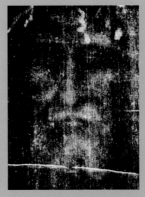
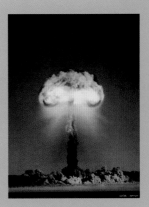

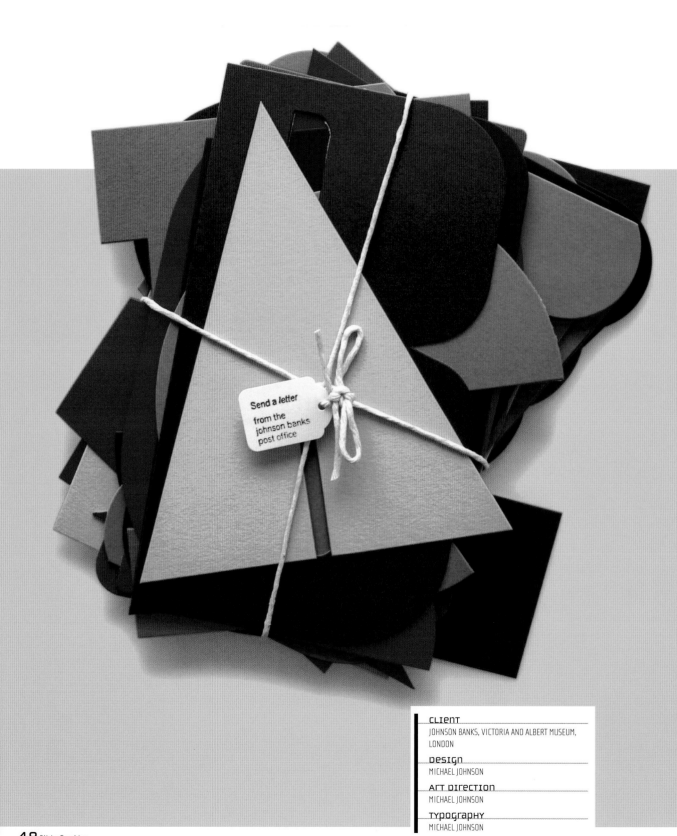

Send a letter

from the
johnson banks
post office

CLIENT
JOHNSON BANKS, VICTORIA AND ALBERT MUSEUM,
LONDON

DESIGN
MICHAEL JOHNSON

ART DIRECTION
MICHAEL JOHNSON

TYPOGRAPHY
MICHAEL JOHNSON

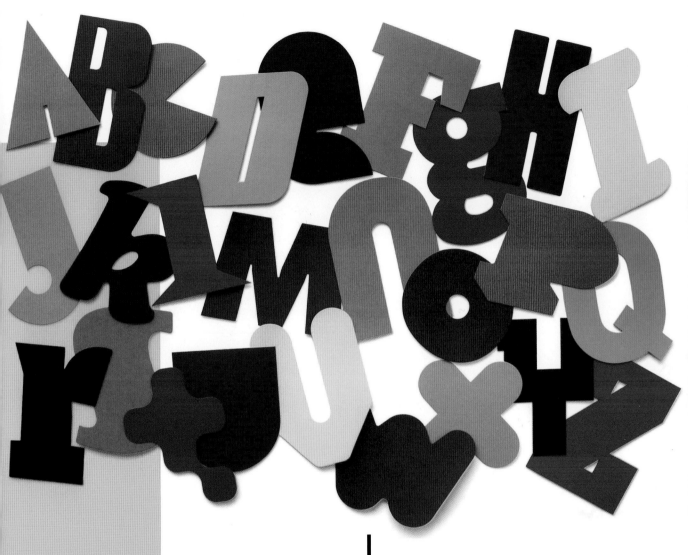

johnson banks

Johnson Banks has created a range of 26 brightly
colored, eye-catching postcards, each individually
shaped as an extra-bold letter of the alphabet. Cards
went on sale at the annual Victoria and Albert Museum
summer event in London, and were mnemonically titled
"Send a Letter." Individually memorable for their bright
colors, chunky shapes, and witty name, the cards are
also irresistible as a set of 26, confronting visitors with
the dilemma of whether to purchase just a few, or the
complete alphabet!

CLIENT
WHITE STUFF

DESIGN
CHRIS LEISHMAN

ART DIRECTION
GEORGE TREVES

Leishman Design

WHITE STUFF SUMMER 2005 CATALOG

Simplistic bold color symbolizes summer in the city on the front and back covers of the White Stuff catalog for summer 2005. The introductory pages to "Girl's Stuff" and "Boy's Stuff" pursue the strong green, white, and yellow theme. Without doubt, the compositions have initial impact and appeal, but they remain in readers' minds because of detailing that stimulates various senses and extends the viewing experience. The introduction of embossing, complementary color, and humor all add to the visual story that makes this catalog memorable.

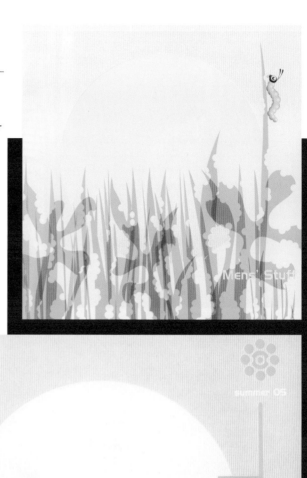

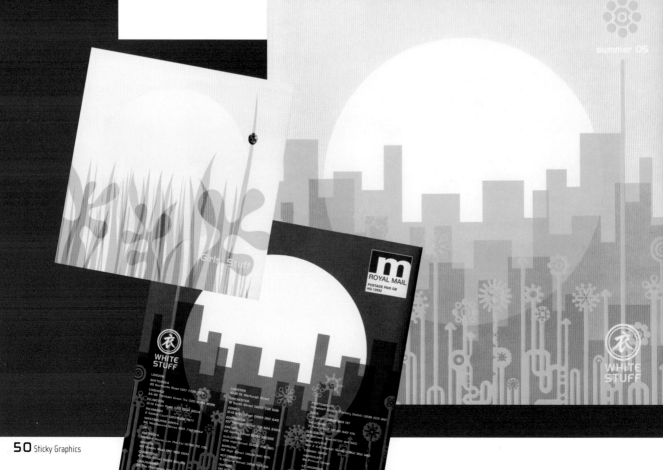

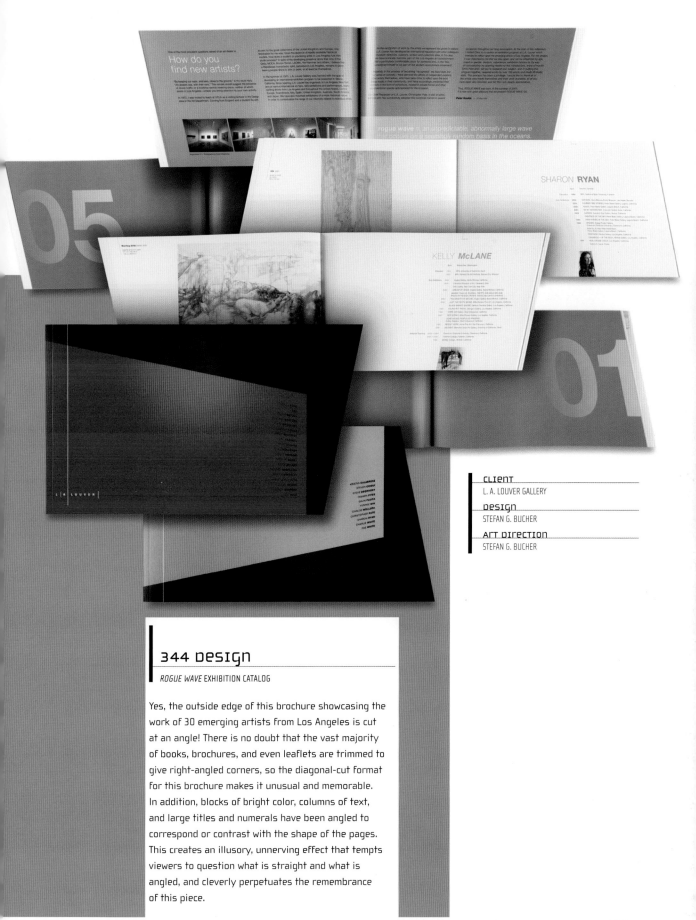

CLIENT
L. A. LOUVER GALLERY
DESIGN
STEFAN G. BUCHER
ART DIRECTION
STEFAN G. BUCHER

344 DESIGN

ROGUE WAVE EXHIBITION CATALOG

Yes, the outside edge of this brochure showcasing the
work of 30 emerging artists from Los Angeles is cut
at an angle! There is no doubt that the vast majority
of books, brochures, and even leaflets are trimmed to
give right-angled corners, so the diagonal-cut format
for this brochure makes it unusual and memorable.
In addition, blocks of bright color, columns of text,
and large titles and numerals have been angled to
correspond or contrast with the shape of the pages.
This creates an illusory, unnerving effect that tempts
viewers to question what is straight and what is
angled, and cleverly perpetuates the remembrance
of this piece.

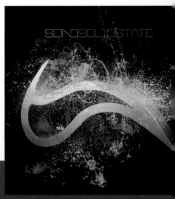

CLIENT	
UNIVERSAL MUSIC	
DESIGN	
DIRK RUDOLPH	
ART DIRECTION	
DIRK RUDOLPH	
PHOTOGRAPHY	
CHRISTOF SCHULTE	
TYPOGRAPHY	
DIRK RUDOLPH	

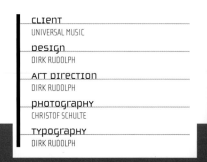

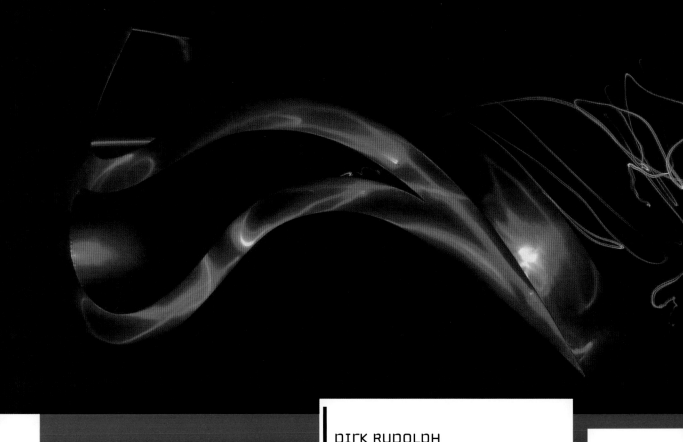

DIRK RUDOLPH

SONO, "SOLID STATE" BOOKLET

The booklet accompanying "Solid State" by Sono, makes terrific use of color, image, and type as image. The small square pages are home to many shots that bleed but that are also embellished with fine, decorative typographic patterning. Images focus on flowers, water splashes, and photographs of the band. The Sono mark is awarded an entire spread, appearing in deep flame red against a black background. Arranged in distinctive, angled groups using narrow columns and wide gutters, lyrics have memorably become image, allowing the viewer to remember not only the words, but also the overall shape and distinctive grouping of the text.

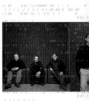

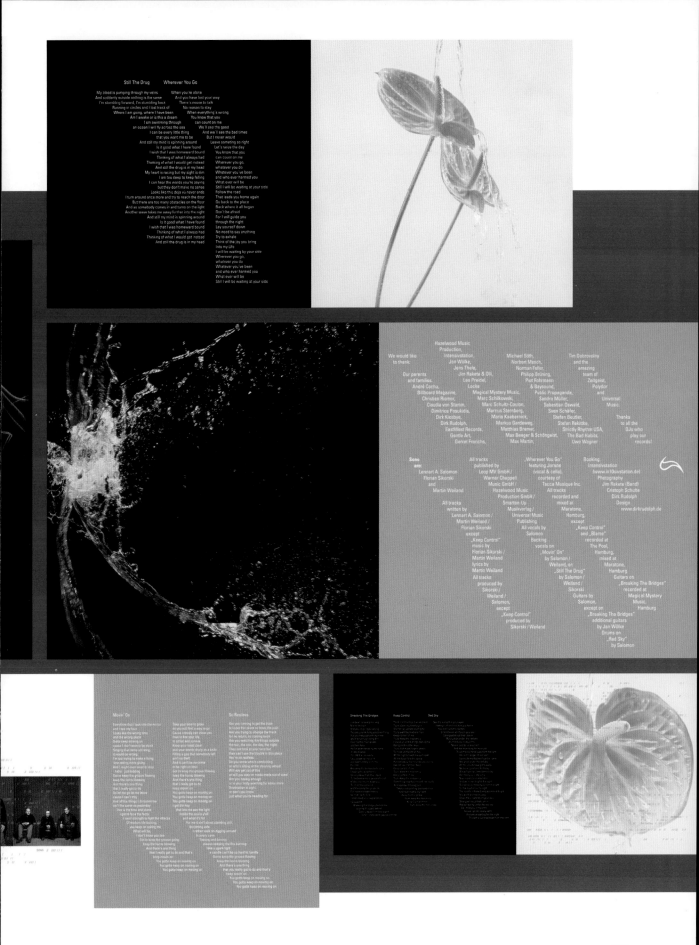

graphic WIT anD SHOCK

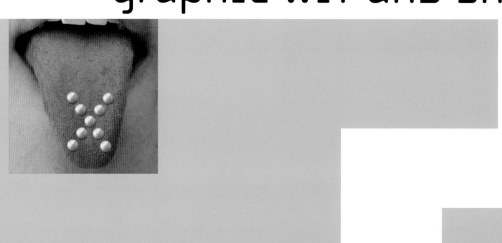

The work in this section showcases examples that demonstrate the use of wit or shock, and have the ability to evoke responses of laughter, amazement, horror, or disgust. Mnemonics require interaction with audiences; they demand that a process takes place, however short, of seeing, understanding, and reacting. Although the reactions to wit and shock are quite different, they are both emotional, successfully and unavoidably extending the viewer's experience, to make it more memorable.

Disconcerting, gruesome, or totally unexpected images, stay in the mind's eye; they are disturbing to viewers, and can remain memorable for a very long time. Audiences are likely to think they have a choice in what they remember or forget, but shocking or raw images can prove unforgettable however hard a viewer tries to eradicate them from memory. It is significant to note that human nature tends to have a fascination with the macabre or unpleasant, and most people have a predisposition to want to discuss disquieting images or information they have seen. This not only perpetuates uncomfortable memories, but also disseminates them to wider "non-seeing" audiences. Similarly, a design that is humorous is tempting to recount, making it memorable for storyteller and listener alike.

section 02

Humor has long been accepted as being helpful in communicating with audiences, as it wraps up information in a relaxed, pleasant, and entertaining manner. There is no doubt that it also can be extremely constructive in enabling the retention of messages. Humor often taps into reality, depicting or at least hinting at experiences with which audiences can identify. This ability to lighten the view on life is appealing and enjoyable, and as a consequence the information it presents is frequently remembered.

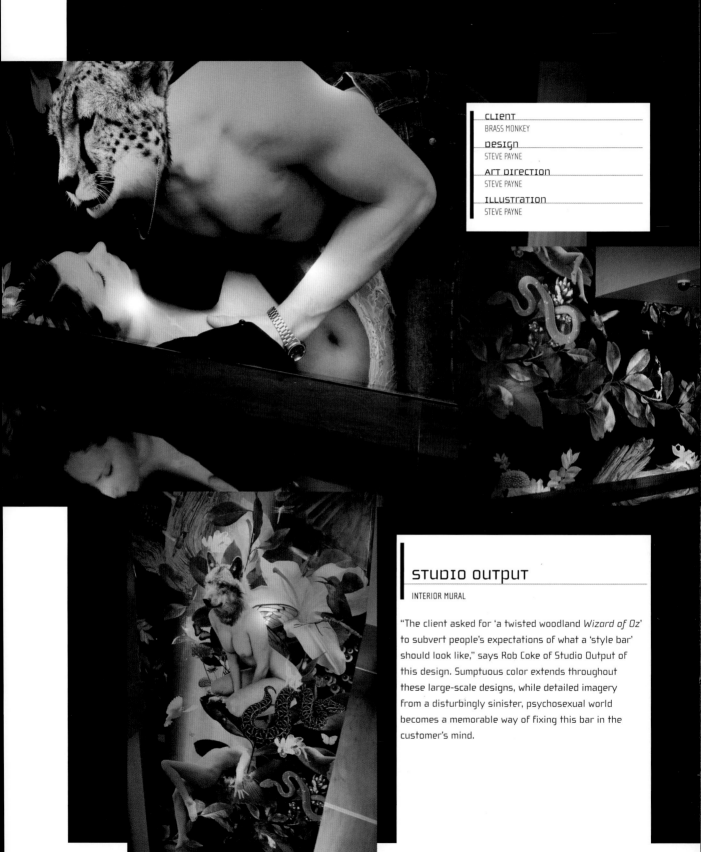

CLIENT
BRASS MONKEY

DESIGN
STEVE PAYNE

ART DIRECTION
STEVE PAYNE

ILLUSTRATION
STEVE PAYNE

STUDIO OUTPUT

INTERIOR MURAL

"The client asked for 'a twisted woodland *Wizard of Oz*' to subvert people's expectations of what a 'style bar' should look like," says Rob Coke of Studio Output of this design. Sumptuous color extends throughout these large-scale designs, while detailed imagery from a disturbingly sinister, psychosexual world becomes a memorable way of fixing this bar in the customer's mind.

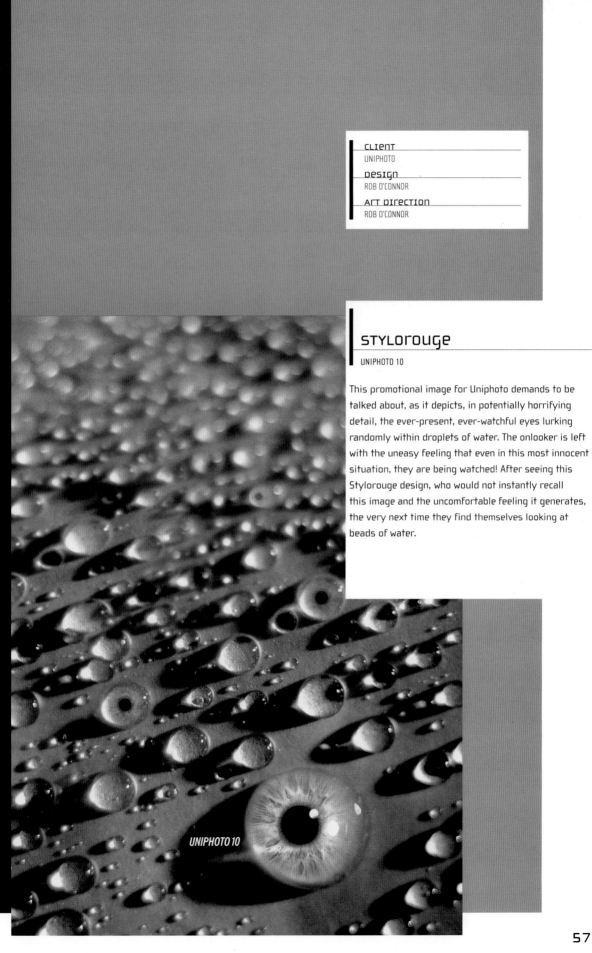

CLIENT	
UNIPHOTO	
DESIGN	
ROB O'CONNOR	
ART DIRECTION	
ROB O'CONNOR	

STYLOROUGE

UNIPHOTO 10

This promotional image for Uniphoto demands to be talked about, as it depicts, in potentially horrifying detail, the ever-present, ever-watchful eyes lurking randomly within droplets of water. The onlooker is left with the uneasy feeling that even in this most innocent situation, they are being watched! After seeing this Stylorouge design, who would not instantly recall this image and the uncomfortable feeling it generates, the very next time they find themselves looking at beads of water.

UNIPHOTO 10

CLIENT
SAKS FIFTH AVENUE
DESIGN
SUE FARRINGTON
ART DIRECTION
GREG QUINTON
PHOTOGRAPHY
STEVE HOSKINS
TYPOGRAPHY
MIKE PRATLEY

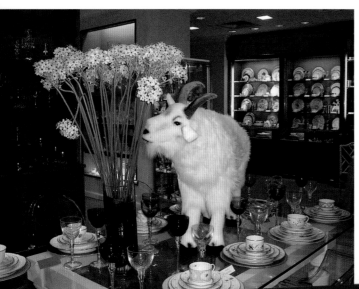

THE PARTNERS

WILD ABOUT CASHMERE

It is not hard to imagine shoppers' responses to a herd of live cashmere goats surging through the doors of Saks in Fifth Avenue, New York. As photographs of the goats, together with life-size cuddly toy goats, are let loose across a range of applications, including catalogs, packaging, window dressings, point of sale, and advertising, they elicit a combination of shock and amusement, that make The Partners campaign, "Wild About Cashmere," both effective and memorable.

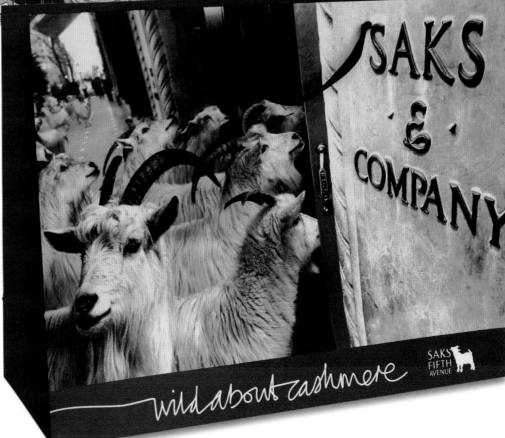

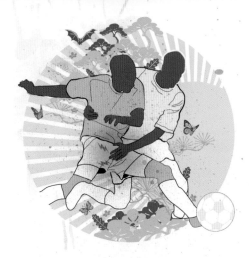

CLIENT
SELF-PROMOTIONAL

DESIGN
REX ADVINCULA

ART DIRECTION
REX ADVINCULA AND JOYCE TAI

ILLUSTRATION
JOYCE TAI

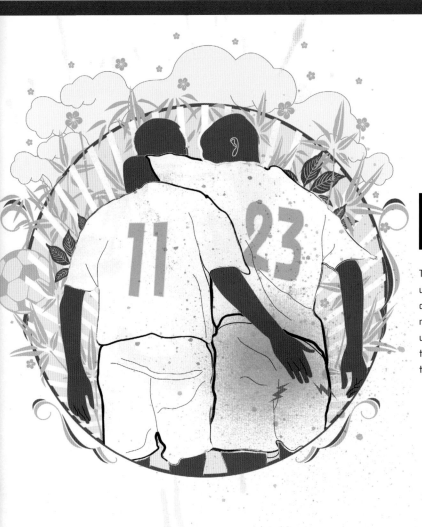

Inksurge

RUGGED THOUGHTS

These self-promotional illustrations for Inksurge use graphic wit and shock to fix the company's strong design and illustration capabilities firmly in the viewer's mind. Images tell a story of an opposing soccer team using "dirty" tactics to gain advantage over the Inksurge team. This narrative also gives the viewer the feeling that there is no area where Inksurge will "fear to tread."

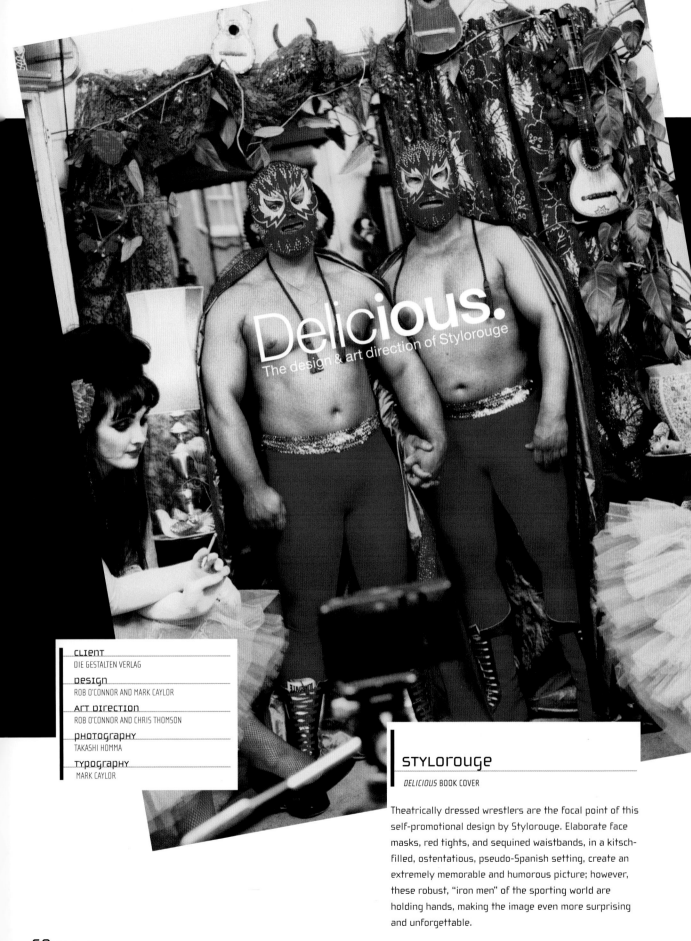

Delicious.
The design & art direction of Stylorouge

CLIENT
DIE GESTALTEN VERLAG

DESIGN
ROB O'CONNOR AND MARK CAYLOR

ART DIRECTION
ROB O'CONNOR AND CHRIS THOMSON

PHOTOGRAPHY
TAKASHI HOMMA

TYPOGRAPHY
MARK CAYLOR

STYLOROUGE

DELICIOUS BOOK COVER

Theatrically dressed wrestlers are the focal point of this self-promotional design by Stylorouge. Elaborate face masks, red tights, and sequined waistbands, in a kitsch-filled, ostentatious, pseudo-Spanish setting, create an extremely memorable and humorous picture; however, these robust, "iron men" of the sporting world are holding hands, making the image even more surprising and unforgettable.

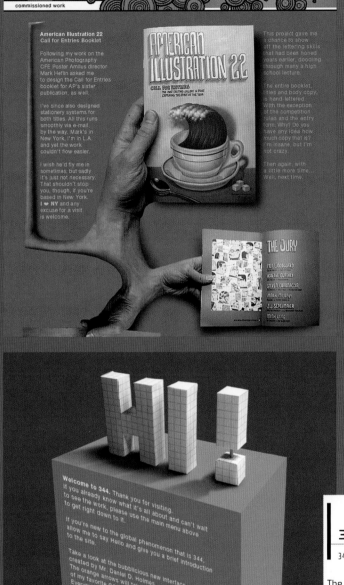

American Illustration 22 Call for Entries Booklet

Following my work on the American Photography CFE Poster Amilus director Mark Heflin asked me to design the Call for Entries booklet for AP's sister publication, as well.

I've since also designed stationery systems for both titles. All this runs smoothly via e-mail, by the way. Mark's in New York, I'm in L.A. and yet the work couldn't flow easier.

I wish he'd fly me in sometimes, but sadly it's just not necessary. That shouldn't stop you, though, if you're based in New York. I ♥ NY and any excuse for a visit is welcome.

This project gave me a chance to show off the lettering skills that had been honed years earlier, doodling through many a high school lecture.

The entire booklet, titles and body copy, is hand-lettered. With the exception of the competition rules and the entry form. Why? Do you have any idea how much copy that is? I'm insane, but I'm not crazy.

Then again, with a little more time... Well, next time.

CLIENT
344 DESIGN

DESIGN
STEFAN G. BUCHER

INTERFACE DESIGN
DANIEL D. HOLMES

344 DESIGN

344 DESIGN WEB SITE

The 344 Design Web site demonstrates Stefan Bucher's very individual sense of humor; following an initial brightly colored animated namestyle, the homepage is a complete contrast, depicting "HI!" in hand-made 3-D letters, perched on top of a plinth. This visual paradox sets the scene for examples of Stefan's distinctive work, including the American Illustration 22 Call for Entries brochure, which is presented by the most extraordinary three-handed limb. Wit and shock are key to much of Stefan's work; this deformity is grotesque, and yet at the same time succeeds in being funny. The combination is so haunting that it makes the image—and the Web site—totally unforgettable.

CLIENT
DDD GALLERY, OSAKA; GGG GALLERY, TOKYO

DESIGN
STEFAN SAGMEISTER AND MATTHIAS ERNSTBERGER

ART DIRECTION
STEFAN SAGMEISTER

PHOTOGRAPHY
TOM SCHIERLITZ

sagmeister inc.

SAGMEISTER ON A BINGE

At first glance, this poster appears to show two slightly different shots of Stefan Sagmeister sitting in his underwear on a couch—undoubtedly, shocking and therefore memorable enough for some viewers. However, the story behind this design is far more haunting and disturbing. The top image shows Stefan weighing 178 pounds; the bottom one shows a weightier Stefan, just one week later, having consumed all the displayed food items, and having gained 25 pounds— "not an enjoyable binge," he reports. The poster is a typical example of subject matter demanding to be discussed and debated, thus perpetuating its mnemonic qualities.

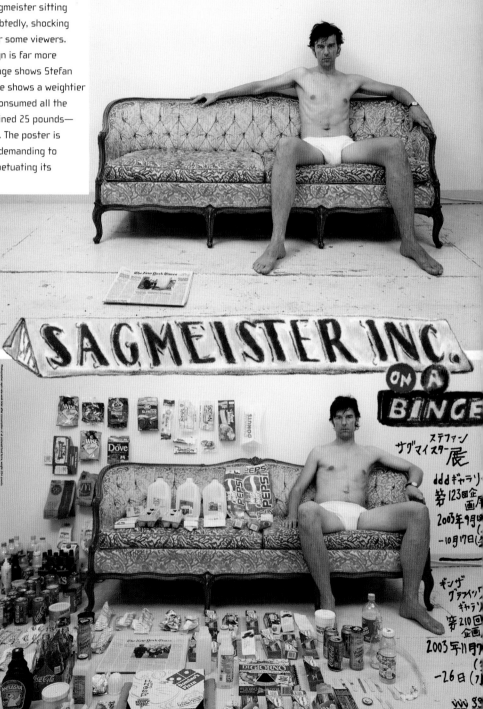

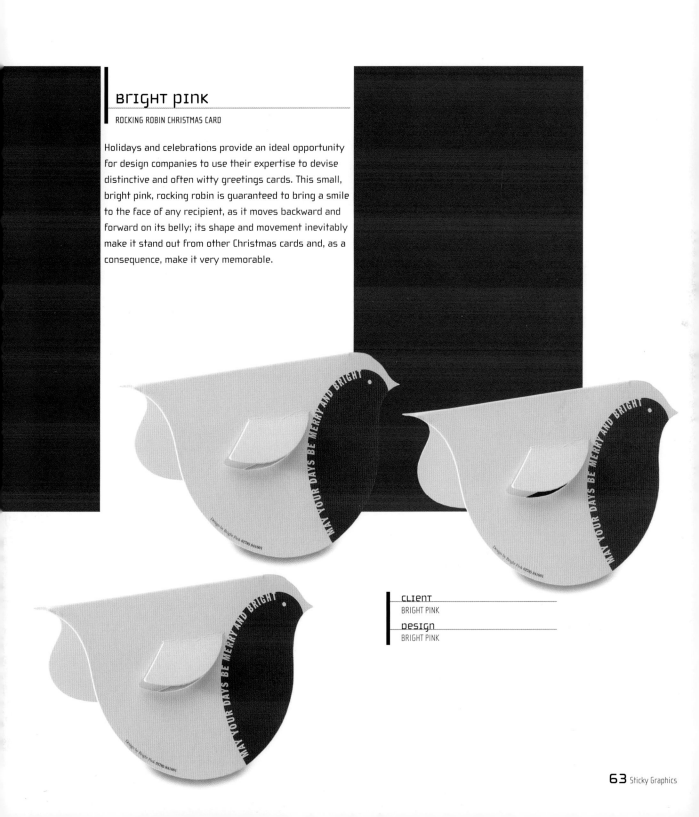

Bright Pink

ROCKING ROBIN CHRISTMAS CARD

Holidays and celebrations provide an ideal opportunity for design companies to use their expertise to devise distinctive and often witty greetings cards. This small, bright pink, rocking robin is guaranteed to bring a smile to the face of any recipient, as it moves backward and forward on its belly; its shape and movement inevitably make it stand out from other Christmas cards and, as a consequence, make it very memorable.

CLIENT
BRIGHT PINK

DESIGN
BRIGHT PINK

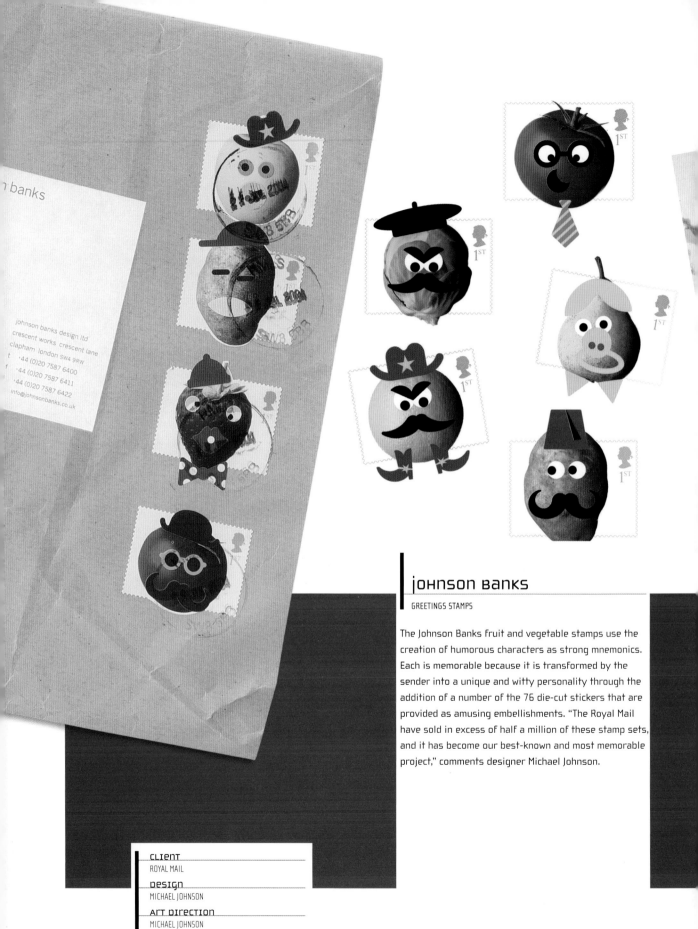

johnson banks

johnson banks design ltd
crescent works crescent lane
clapham london SW4 9RW
t   +44 (0)20 7587 6400
    +44 (0)20 7587 6411
f   +44 (0)20 7587 6422
info@johnsonbanks.co.uk

johnson banks

GREETINGS STAMPS

The Johnson Banks fruit and vegetable stamps use the creation of humorous characters as strong mnemonics. Each is memorable because it is transformed by the sender into a unique and witty personality through the addition of a number of the 76 die-cut stickers that are provided as amusing embellishments. "The Royal Mail have sold in excess of half a million of these stamp sets, and it has become our best-known and most memorable project," comments designer Michael Johnson.

CLIENT
ROYAL MAIL

DESIGN
MICHAEL JOHNSON

ART DIRECTION
MICHAEL JOHNSON

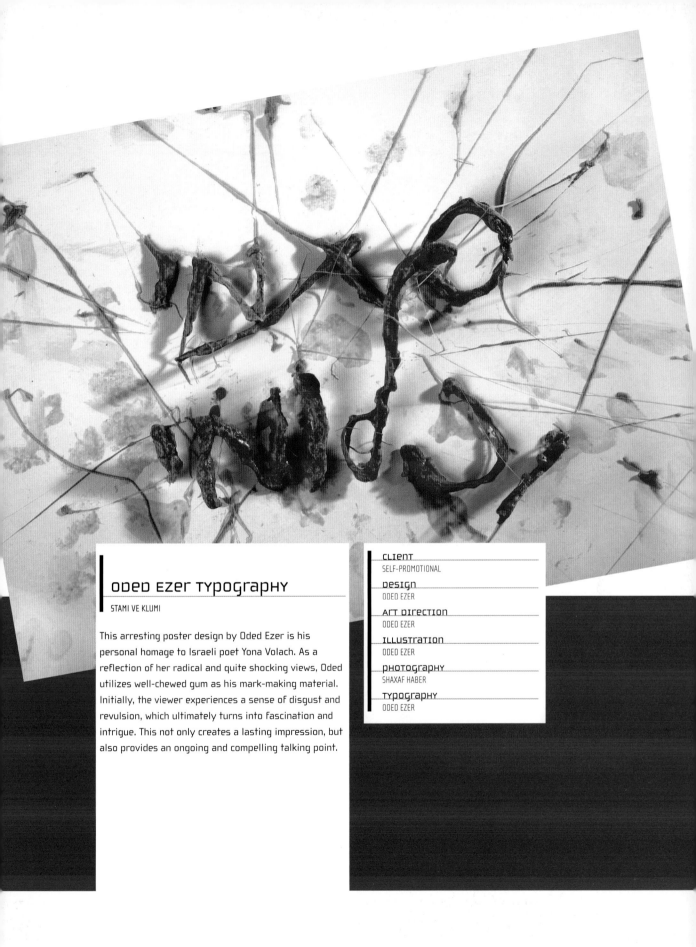

ODED EZER TYPOGRAPHY

STAMI VE KLUMI

This arresting poster design by Oded Ezer is his personal homage to Israeli poet Yona Volach. As a reflection of her radical and quite shocking views, Oded utilizes well-chewed gum as his mark-making material. Initially, the viewer experiences a sense of disgust and revulsion, which ultimately turns into fascination and intrigue. This not only creates a lasting impression, but also provides an ongoing and compelling talking point.

CLIENT
SELF-PROMOTIONAL

DESIGN
ODED EZER

ART DIRECTION
ODED EZER

ILLUSTRATION
ODED EZER

PHOTOGRAPHY
SHAXAF HABER

TYPOGRAPHY
ODED EZER

STYLOROUGE

100% PURE STYLOROUGE PROMOTIONAL T-SHIRT

At first glance, this image of a green cow, created by Rob O'Connor of Stylorouge, seems unusual and attention-grabbing in itself; after all, there aren't many green cows about. However, when going back for a second look, the viewer becomes aware that its markings, which would usually be irregular black and white areas, are in fact a map of the world. The unexpected synthesis of cow, green, and world map make this image humorous and totally unforgettable.

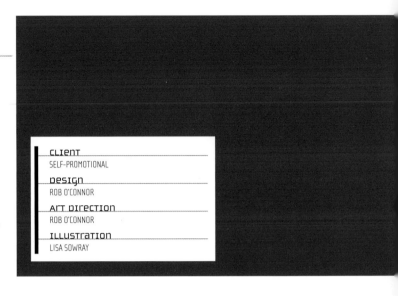

CLIENT
SELF-PROMOTIONAL

DESIGN
ROB O'CONNOR

ART DIRECTION
ROB O'CONNOR

ILLUSTRATION
LISA SOWRAY

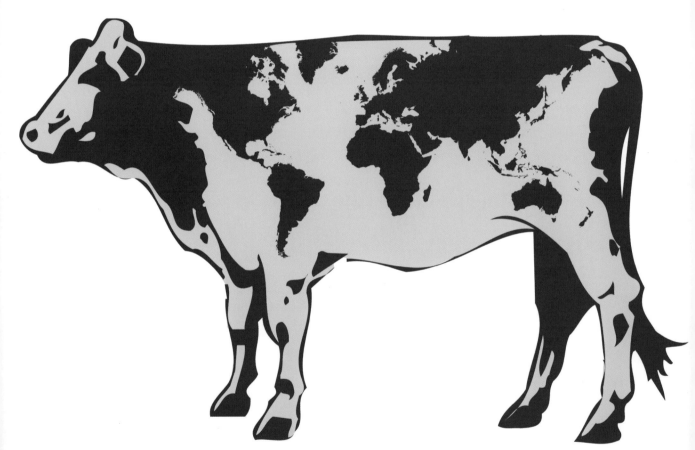

100% pure Stylo**rouge.**

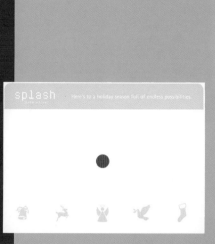

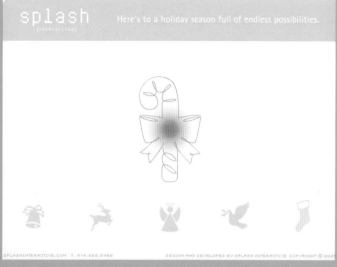

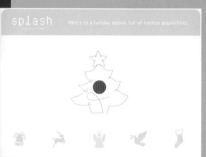

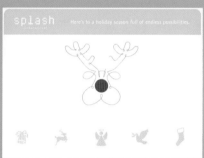

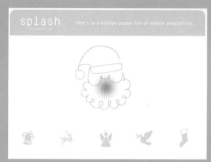

splash interactive

2005 CHRISTMAS GREETINGS

Christmas greetings from Splash Interactive in
December 2005 were sent interactively, allowing
the recipient to progress enjoyably through the five
areas of this mnemonic greeting. Viewers click onto
the selected icon and then experience an associated
illustration building before their eyes and around the
red dot in the center of their screen. If the humor of
this experience were not memorable enough, each
animated illustration forms in time to a catchy tune
that is guaranteed to stay in the forefront of the
viewer's mind—if they can stop humming, that is!

CLIENT	SELF-PROMOTIONAL
DESIGN	IVY WONG
ART DIRECTION	IVY WONG
COPYWRITING	LISA SOWRAY
FLASH DEVELOPER	IVY WONG
TYPOGRAPHY	IVY WONG

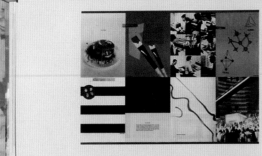

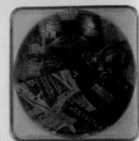
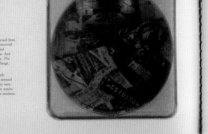

CLIENT
RHINO

DESIGN
MATTHIAS ERNSTBERGER

ART DIRECTION
STEFAN SAGMEISTER

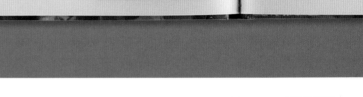
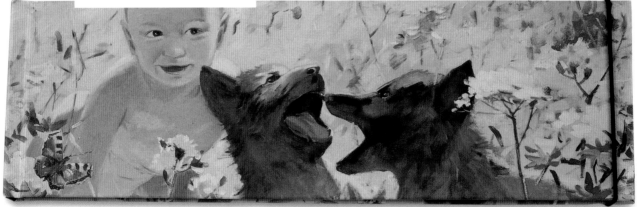
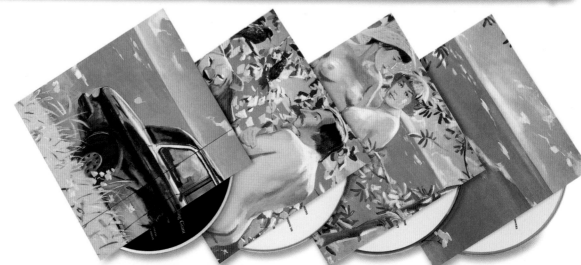

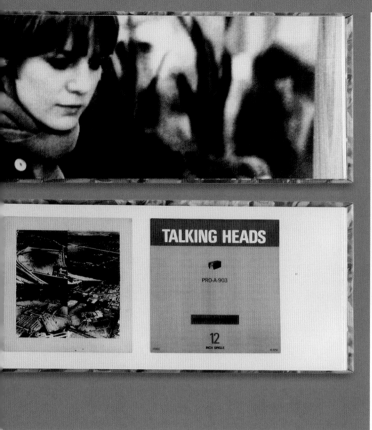

sagmeister inc.

TALKING HEADS CD PACKAGING

"Surely, a truly witty and memorable CD design has to feature a bear, a dismembered limb, and a naked person," says Stefan Sagmeister. His design for Talking Heads' "Once in a Lifetime" boxed set has just this and more, namely three bears, 12 frolicking nude bodies, and a number of severed body parts. The unusual, elongated panoramic format of this piece is easy to store, but also does a very good job in obstructing all CDs stored behind it, making "Once in a Lifetime" unforgettable and difficult to ignore.

PAULMsCartney

stylorouge

PAUL MCCARTNEY AMBIGRAM

This fascinating, surprising, and memorable namestyle for Paul McCartney is known as an "ambigram." "Ambi" means "both" and signifies that this group of letters can be read both ways round, without any compromise to legibility. It is particularly memorable because the principle of ambigrams is very clever and very difficult to achieve, making the experience for readers a subtle combination of enjoyment and appreciation.

CLIENT
PAUL MCCARTNEY, MPL

DESIGN
ROB O'CONNOR AND ANTHONY LUI

TYPOGRAPHY
ROB O'CONNOR AND ANTHONY LUI

CLIENT
MINISTRY OF SOUND, LONDON

DESIGN
STEVE PAYNE

ART DIRECTION
STEVE PAYNE

ILLUSTRATION
STEVE PAYNE

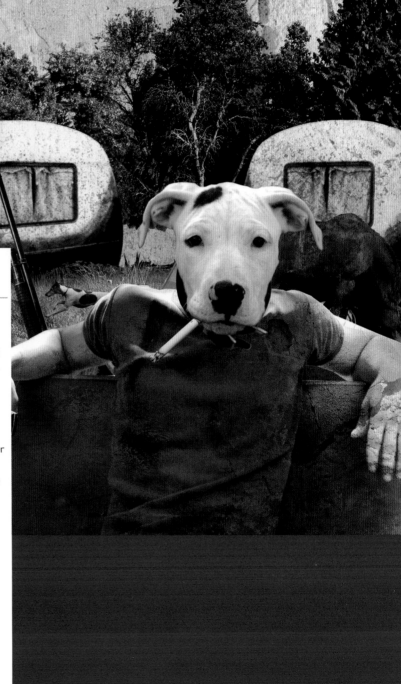

STUDIO OUTPUT

MINISTRY OF SOUND INTERIOR GRAPHICS

"We were asked to design some interior panels to fit within the new decor at Ministry of Sound, to be called 'Ministry Manor,'" says Rob Coke of Studio Output. "We decided on the theme of 'poacher turned gamekeeper,' sitting these striking giant panels within ornate gold frames." Strange, tormenting photomontage creations show superimposed heads of hunted and hunting animals on the shoulders of human hunters. The viewer is memorably caught directly in the gaze of these animals, and, in one instance, disturbingly fixed at the end of the barrel of this strange creature's gun.

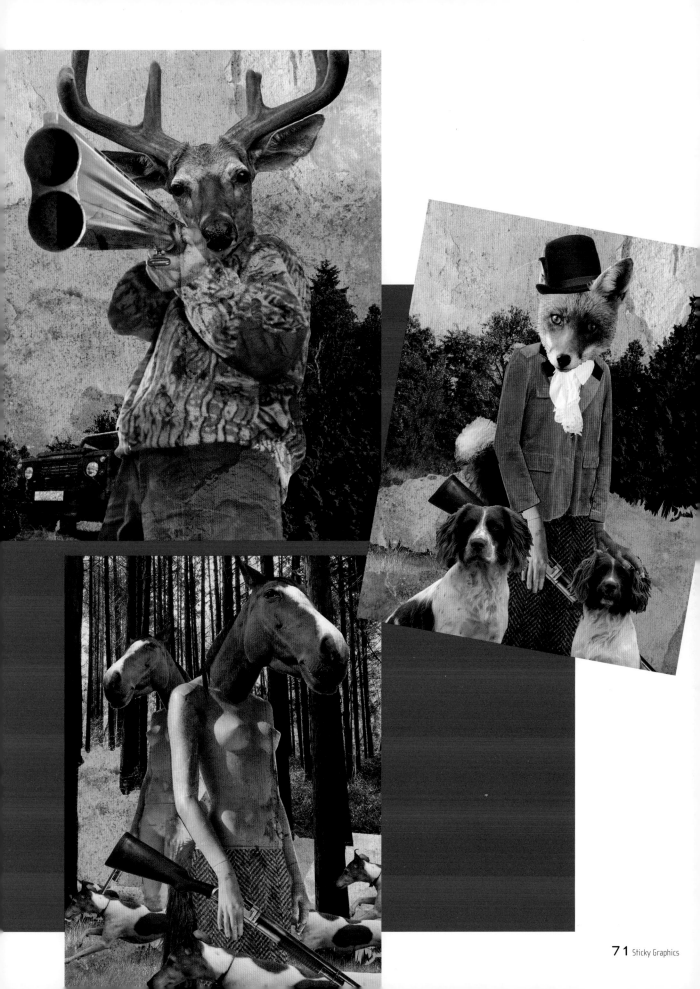

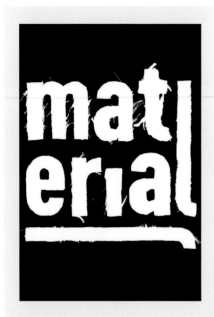

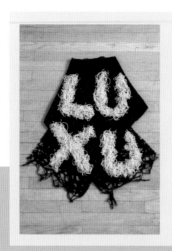

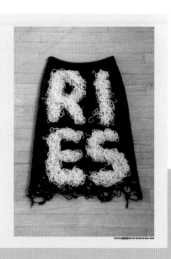

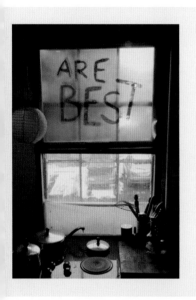

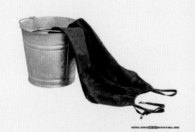

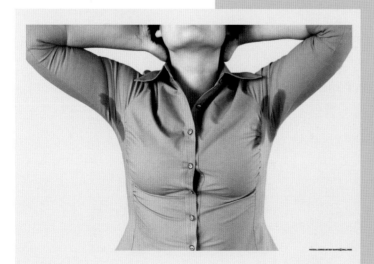

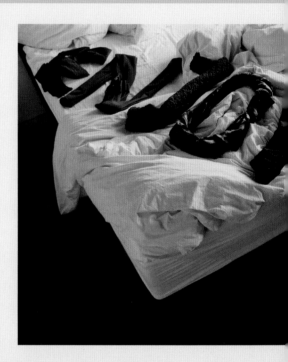

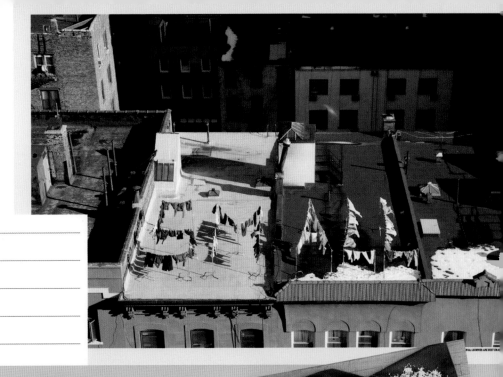

CLIENT
ANNI KUAN

DESIGN
ARIANE SPIRANNI

ART DIRECTION
STEFAN SAGMEISTER

ILLUSTRATION
ARIANE SPIRANNI

PHOTOGRAPHY
ARIANE SPIRANNI

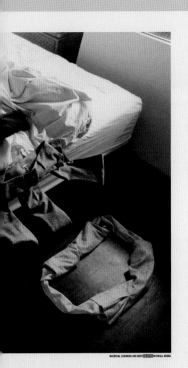

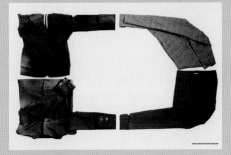

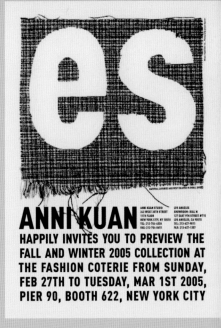

sagmeister inc.

ANNI KUAN "GOLD" BROCHURE

This unexpected combination of generally unconnected elements creates a whimsical theme for Anni Kuan's brochure entitled "Gold." Each letter in the sentence "Material luxuries are best enjoyed in small doses," is created with the help of one of Anni's garments, establishing a clever and amusing series of images that are quite unforgettable. "And yes, that is real, actual gold on the front cover (albeit a small dose)," says art director Stefan Sagmeister.

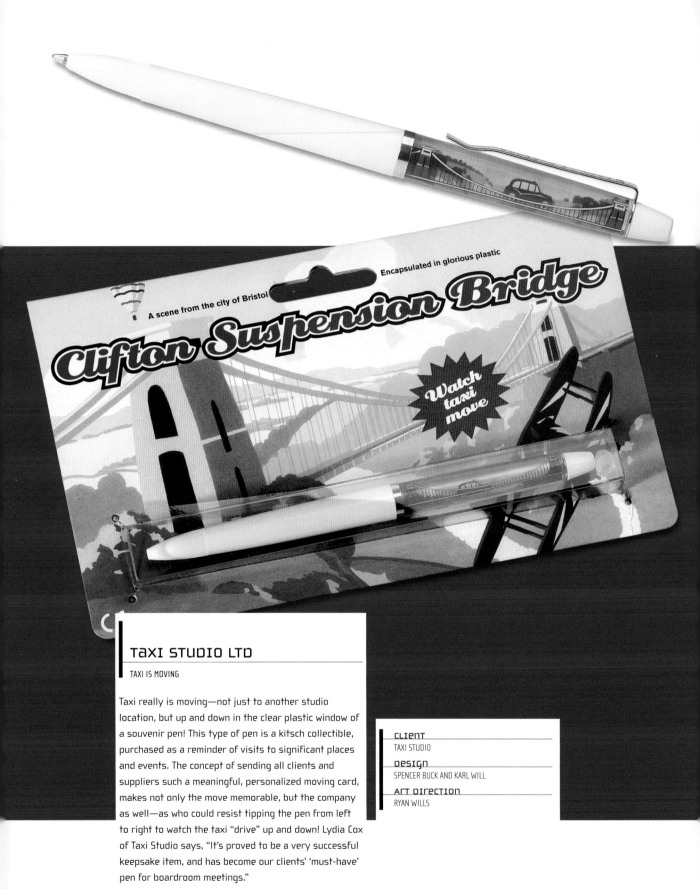

TAXI STUDIO LTD

TAXI IS MOVING

Taxi really is moving—not just to another studio location, but up and down in the clear plastic window of a souvenir pen! This type of pen is a kitsch collectible, purchased as a reminder of visits to significant places and events. The concept of sending all clients and suppliers such a meaningful, personalized moving card, makes not only the move memorable, but the company as well—as who could resist tipping the pen from left to right to watch the taxi "drive" up and down! Lydia Cox of Taxi Studio says, "It's proved to be a very successful keepsake item, and has become our clients' 'must-have' pen for boardroom meetings."

CLIENT
TAXI STUDIO

DESIGN
SPENCER BUCK AND KARL WILL

ART DIRECTION
RYAN WILLS

Before I began my research for this essay, I was inclined to connect Heard's work with the Mannerist sensibility that followed the High Renaissance, precisely because it was an aesthetic that encapsulated and heightened the anxiety of the times, much as Heard's art does. In his authoritative volume, Mannerism, the eminent social art historian, Arnold Hauser, documents the way that this hermetic and expressive sensibility evolved out of the social ferment of the latter half of the sixteenth century. The establishment of the first great bureaucracies (religious, financial and governmental) also created a new skepticism and alienation in the broader populace. Waves of plagues and venereal diseases created great anxieties about the body and mortality, and a fascination with the grotesque often comes to the fore in such periods. Symptomatic of the polarized tenor of times, this era is the birth of modern atheism in response to the new discoveries in astronomy that contradicted the Church of Rome's teachings, yet another portion of society turned to an impassioned piety that was much more intense than the more secular instincts of the Renaissance. This devotion becomes apparent when comparing the radiant religiosity of Mannerists El Greco and Tintoretto to the sensuous corporeality of Michelangelo or Botticelli.

However a pressing question arose during my research about the interrelations of the Gothic, Mannerist and Surreal, as many of the texts to which I turned mentioned this weave of sensibilities. Why should they share characteristics when they are separated by centuries and the social circumstances of each period seem so wildly different? Pondering this puzzle, I came to a startling conclusion. If the Mannerists were Gothic artists with the lessons of perspective and anatomy under their belt, even if they perversely chose to ignore many of those skills, then the Surrealists were Mannerists given a good dollop of modernist aesthetics and Freudian psychoanalytic theory while, once again, perversely forsaking one or both. Anxious eras are times of great flux, where technological innovations create a

significant shift in the paradigms of the society. The invention of the printing press did this in the sixteenth century just as the inception of the internet has profoundly affected our times. A consequence of the press was a proliferation of images- wood engravings in printed books- to satisfy public curiosity about freakish, monstrous bodies: Siamese twins, three legged men, bearded women, cyclopes, and a myriad of other mutants. All embodied the corporal anxiety of the era, inflamed as it was by plagues and new venereal diseases. Heard, in past bodies of work has explored the mutation of Siamese twins and the intrusion of death into the erotic. The cranium and skeleton is invariably suggested beneath the skin of Heard's figures, creating omens of contemporary health threats like AIDS, Ebola and drug-resistant TB that have created great panic in both the media and the body politic.

The recent cinematic obsession with cyborgs, human replicas, and clones in films like Blade Runner and A.I. reveal our own sense that the body in the computer age is becoming less substantial, more hypothetical. There are two ways that Mannerism renders the body insubstantial: in the northern Mannerism of Brueghal, the bodies become ciphers, stubby surrogates in the service of his narratives of his morality tales. In the southern Mannerism of Italy and Spain the figure is abstracted and distorted through elongation, twisted into the infamous "figura serpentina" in order to express personal agony and alienation or spiritual ethereality. In the Gothic the body becomes a conduit for disincarnate notions of spirituality. We never see a desiring corporal being in the Gothic, we see serene or tortured figurines playing out the spiritual ideologies of their times. In Breton's surrealism we see the body as desiring vessel, emptied out and distorted for the artist's libidinal pleasure. However, the distortion of the figures in Catherine Heard's work relates primarily to the dual intent of Mannerism: they become pliable entities in the service of her narratives while (in seeming contradiction) they mirror both inner and societal crisis.

CLIENT
MEDICINE HAT MUSEUM AND ART GALLERY

DESIGN
KELLY HARTMAN AND GILES WOODWARD

ART DIRECTION
KELLY HARTMAN AND GILES WOODWARD

COPYWRITING
ANDY FABO AND JOANNE MARION

TYPOGRAPHY
KELLY HARTMAN AND GILES WOODWARD

FISHTEN DESIGN

CATHERINE HEARD, *EFFLORESCENCE & ID*

Red embroidered typography on a white fabric cover makes the initial impact of this catalog unique and unforgettable; however, as the reader begins to understand its origins, a more complex and deep-seated response of wonder combined with revulsion takes over, leaving a far more lasting impression. The lettering parallels Catherine Heard's art installation, which shows dolls and fabric with attached limbs, intricately embroidered with red pocks that spread and develop into flowers and tendrils. A number of unusual elements occur throughout the catalog, but the most disturbing mirrors the pocks and rashes, with red "blotches" of type building across the text.

catherine heard efflorescence

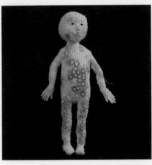 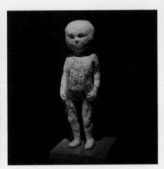

Efflorescence installation detail, 1997   photo: Simon Glass   *Efflorescence installation detail, 1997   photo: Simon Glass*

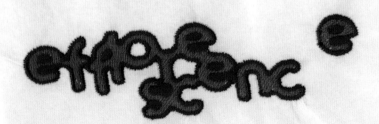

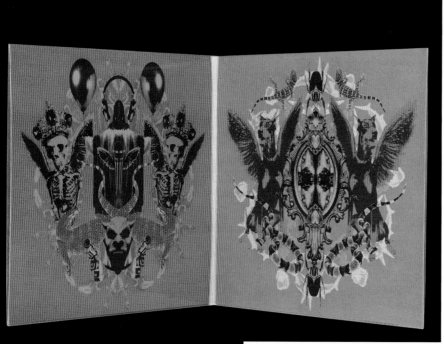

zion graphics

THOMAS RUSIAK

With a fleeting glance, or from a distance, this CD design for Thomas Rusiak looks as if it features brightly colored heraldic crests. This would be memorable enough (as historic coats of arms are not usually noted for their use of garish hues) were it not for the fact that the viewer is led to the shocking revelation that the crests are made up of a fantastic mix of disturbing creatures and dangerous weapons. The combination of acidic bright colors with visions of nightmares or phobias guarantees to captivate the viewer and firmly affix Zion's design in the memory.

CLIENT
S56

DESIGN
RICKY TILLBLAD

ART DIRECTION
RICKY TILLBLAD

TYPOGRAPHY
RICKY TILLBLAD

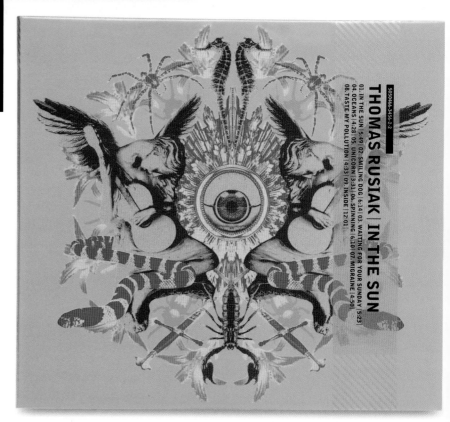

ᴣᴣrpm

JOHN IN THE MORNING AT NIGHT KEXP BENEFIT POSTERS

These posters by 33rpm amusingly and memorably promote an evening benefit hosted by John Richards, the morning DJ for Seattle radio station KEXP. Designer Andrio Abero has created a mnemonic series that features two listeners of the morning show. However, the two radio fans are blue-skinned and have orange hair; they suffer from terrible bags under their eyes and are having a really "bad hair day!" By using great exaggeration, Andrio has ensured that his designs, and therefore the benefit, will be talked about and remembered by all who see them.

CLIENT
KEXP, SEATTLE

DESIGN
ANDRIO ABERO

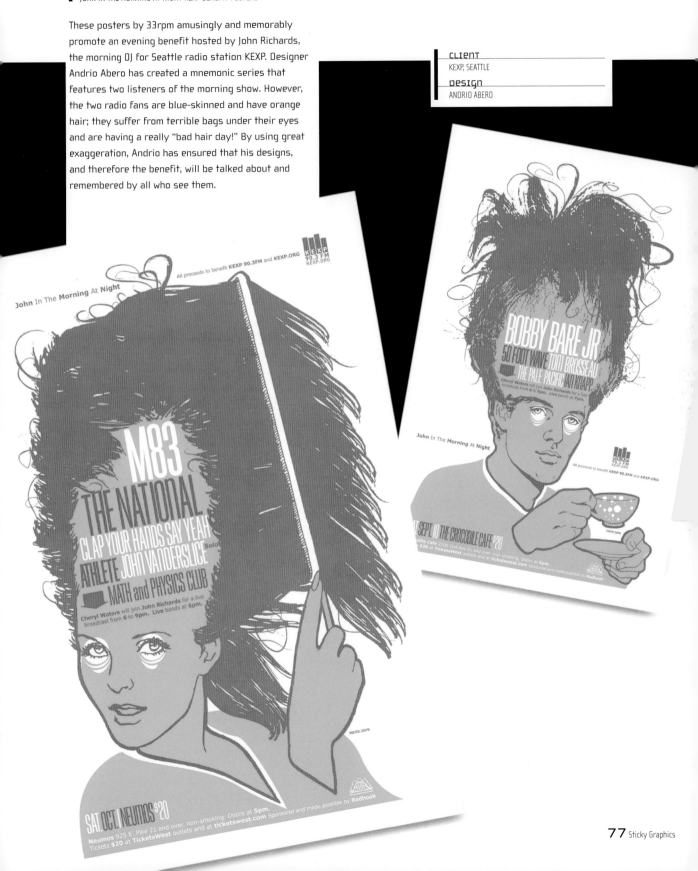

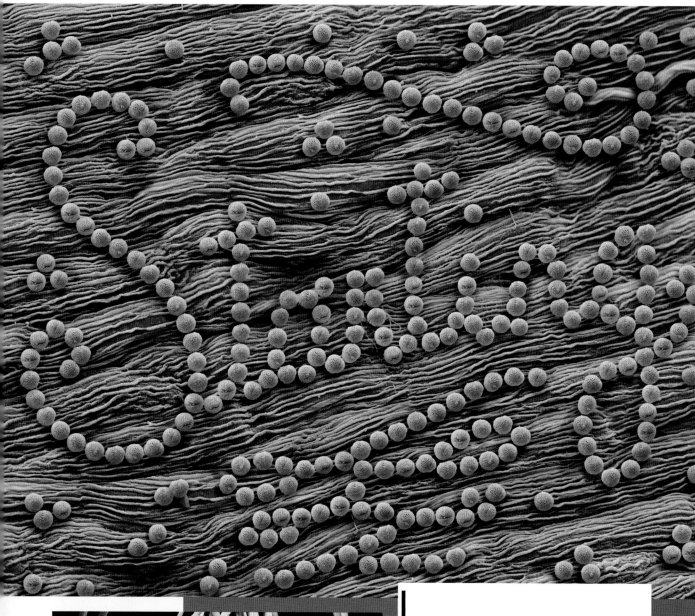

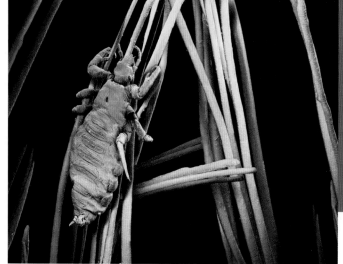

sagmeister inc.

The viewer is treated to a startling and rare glimpse of a colorful microscopic world within these dividing pages for Austrian magazine *.Copy*. Impactful, mnemonic letterforms and words are created by the coming together of microbes, in a manner that initially manifests as purely decorative, but transpires to be hugely magnified scientific detail. The viewer's transition from considering images to be jewellike and simply decorative, to realizing that the photography portrays thousands and thousands of minuscule living organisms in larger-than-life detail, is the process that makes these designs particularly memorable.

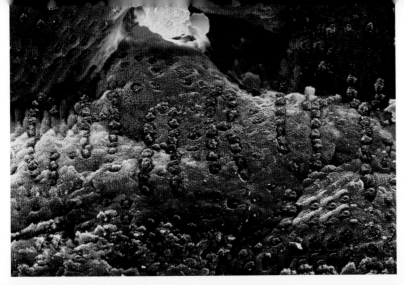

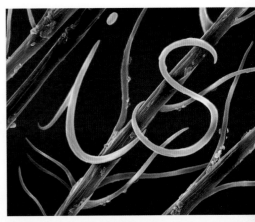

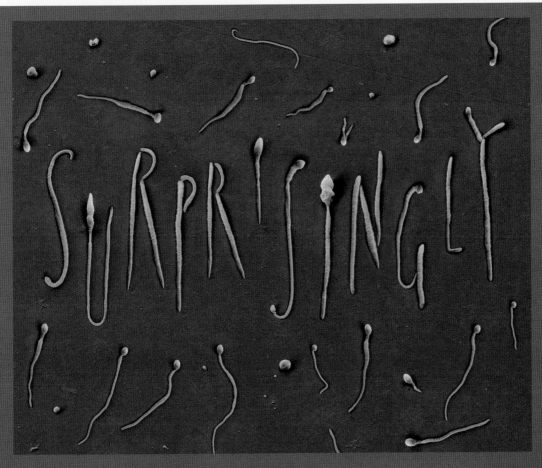

CLIENT
.*COPY* MAGAZINE, AUSTRIA

DESIGN
TRAIAN STANESCU

ART DIRECTION
STEFAN SAGMEISTER

PHOTOGRAPHY
OLIVER MECKES AND NICOLE OTTAWA

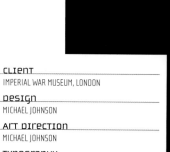

CLIENT
IMPERIAL WAR MUSEUM, LONDON

DESIGN
MICHAEL JOHNSON

ART DIRECTION
MICHAEL JOHNSON

TYPOGRAPHY
MICHAEL JOHNSON

JOHNSON BANKS

WORLD WAR I REMEMBERED

The bright red poppy has become an enduring symbol commemorating World War I; the delicate flower sprang up from the fields of death, and is now forever associated with the tragic loss of young life. Johnson Banks has used this fragile flower as the centerpiece for its poster design for the Imperial War Museum, London, marking the 80th anniversary of the end of World War I. This association is instantly understandable and memorable; however, there is a clever, unexpected, and highly mnemonic twist to this design, in the form of a knot, symbolizing "never forget," in the flower's thin green stem.

An exhibition commemorating the eightieth anniversary of the end of the First World War. 18 September – 28 December 1998 Imperial War Museum ↔ Lambeth North or Elephant and Castle For exhibition information and details of associated special events tel 0171 416 5000 www.iwm.org.uk

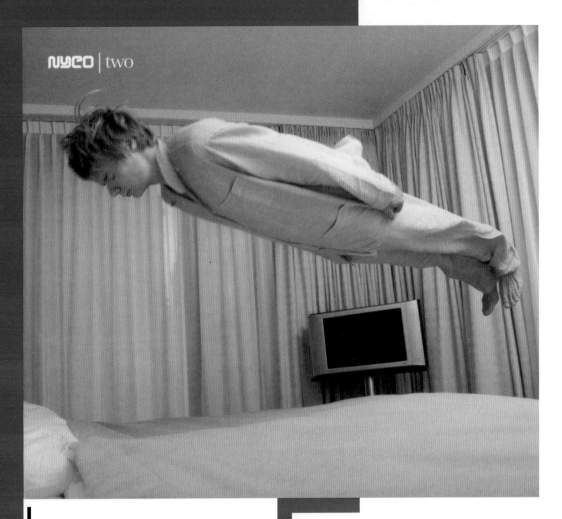

NYCO | two

MPERIAL WAR

MUSEUM

segura inc.

NYCO TWO

When photographic images capture unusual or
unexpected moments in time, they stick in the
mind's eye, and both the front- and the back-cover
photographs on this CD fall into this category. However,
they become really memorable as they haunt the viewer,
who slowly realizes that it would be impossible for the
two figures featured to be in such unusual positions!
Both shots must have been cunningly manipulated,
rotating the figures from vertical positions to horizontal,
creating subtle illusions that set these unforgettable
images apart.

CLIENT
THICKFACE RECORDS

DESIGN
CARLOS SEGURA

ART DIRECTION
CARLOS SEGURA

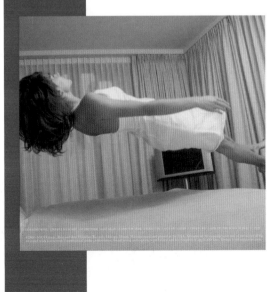

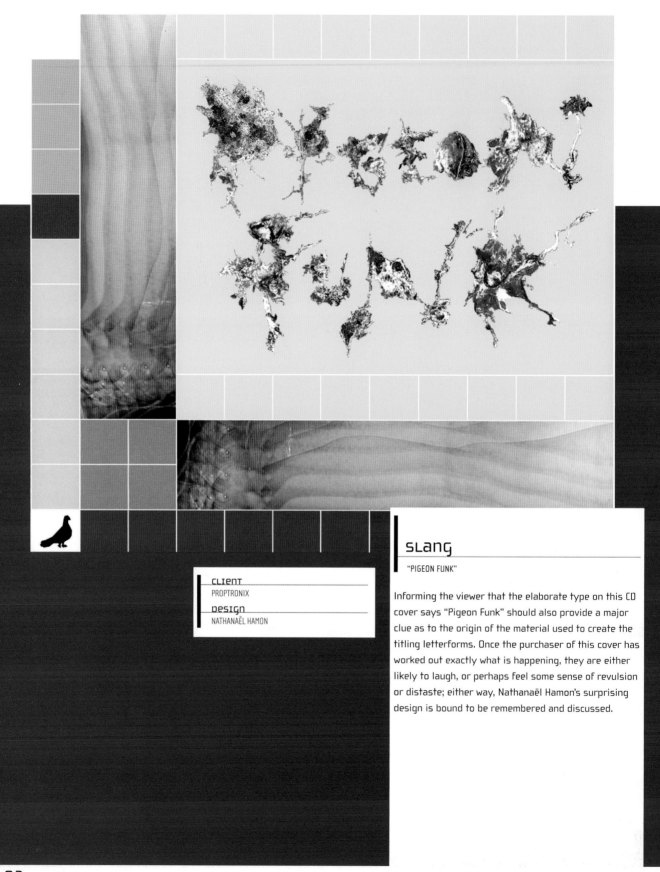

slang

"PIGEON FUNK"

Informing the viewer that the elaborate type on this CD cover says "Pigeon Funk" should also provide a major clue as to the origin of the material used to create the titling letterforms. Once the purchaser of this cover has worked out exactly what is happening, they are either likely to laugh, or perhaps feel some sense of revulsion or distaste; either way, Nathanaël Hamon's surprising design is bound to be remembered and discussed.

CLIENT
PROPTRONIX
DESIGN
NATHANAËL HAMON

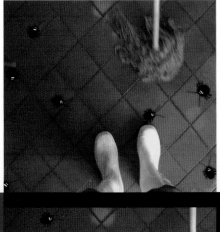

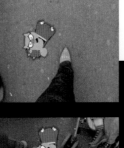

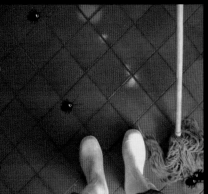

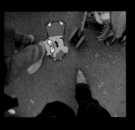

AIRSIDE

MTV MOBILE TV

The humorous interplay of dynamic photography and flat-color illustration constructs a number of visual narratives for MTV Mobile TV that are extremely appealing and memorable. Unusual and distinctive angles of photography, skillfully and amusingly combined with brightly colored illustrations, create simple yet quirky animations that make viewers laugh, and want to play them over and over again.

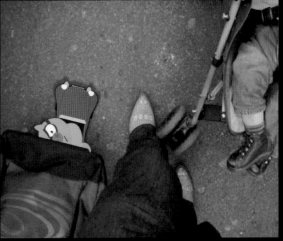

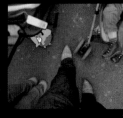

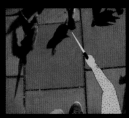

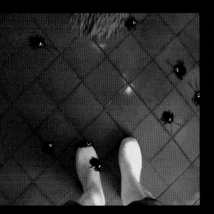

CLIENT
MTV NETWORKS INTERNATIONAL

DESIGN
AIRSIDE

ILLUSTRATION
AIRSIDE

PHOTOGRAPHY
AIRSIDE

TYPOGRAPHY
AIRSIDE

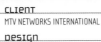

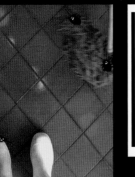

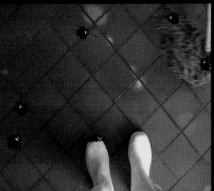

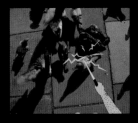

344 DESIGN

344 FLOWERS POSTER

Stefan Bucher created this poster to send out to his friends and clients to celebrate the beginning of spring. However, the plants are growing and blooming with a show of 344 faces instead of flowers, and every face is different! In an age where technology and digital imaging enable simple cloning and manipulation, viewers feel convinced that there might be repetitions. As they move from face to face, however, it is clear that all have been individually drawn; the characters take on familiar personalities, and the poster becomes more and more amusing, distinctive, and memorable.

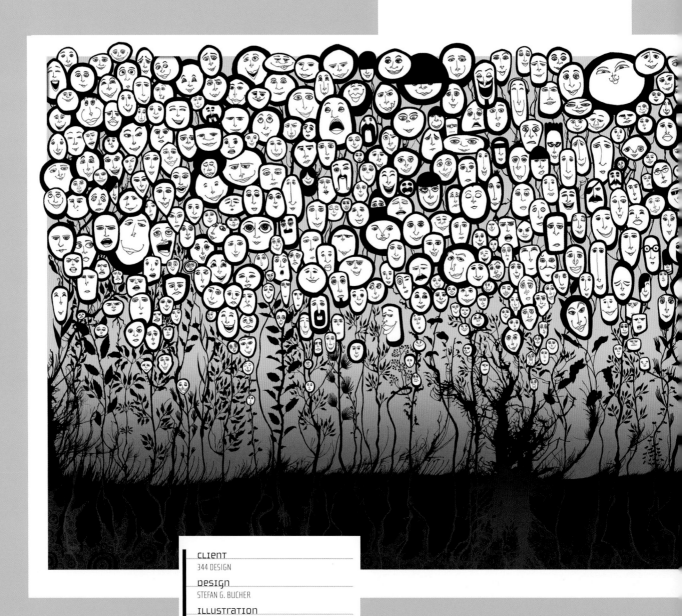

CLIENT
344 DESIGN

DESIGN
STEFAN G. BUCHER

ILLUSTRATION
STEFAN G. BUCHER

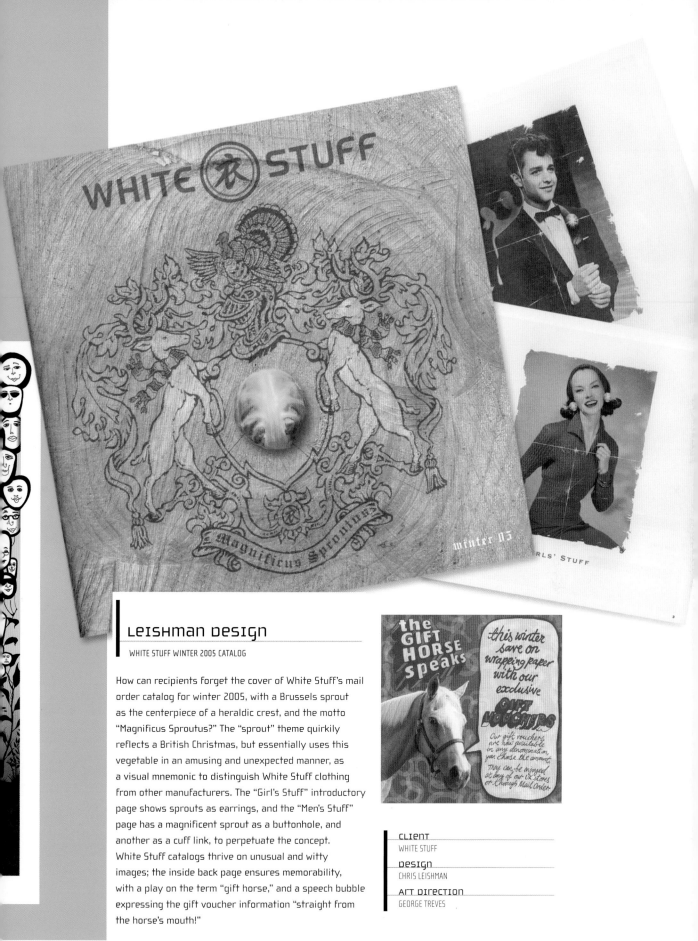

leishman design

WHITE STUFF WINTER 2005 CATALOG

How can recipients forget the cover of White Stuff's mail order catalog for winter 2005, with a Brussels sprout as the centerpiece of a heraldic crest, and the motto "Magnificus Sproutus?" The "sprout" theme quirkily reflects a British Christmas, but essentially uses this vegetable in an amusing and unexpected manner, as a visual mnemonic to distinguish White Stuff clothing from other manufacturers. The "Girl's Stuff" introductory page shows sprouts as earrings, and the "Men's Stuff" page has a magnificent sprout as a buttonhole, and another as a cuff link, to perpetuate the concept. White Stuff catalogs thrive on unusual and witty images; the inside back page ensures memorability, with a play on the term "gift horse," and a speech bubble expressing the gift voucher information "straight from the horse's mouth!"

CLIENT
WHITE STUFF

DESIGN
CHRIS LEISHMAN

ART DIRECTION
GEORGE TREVES

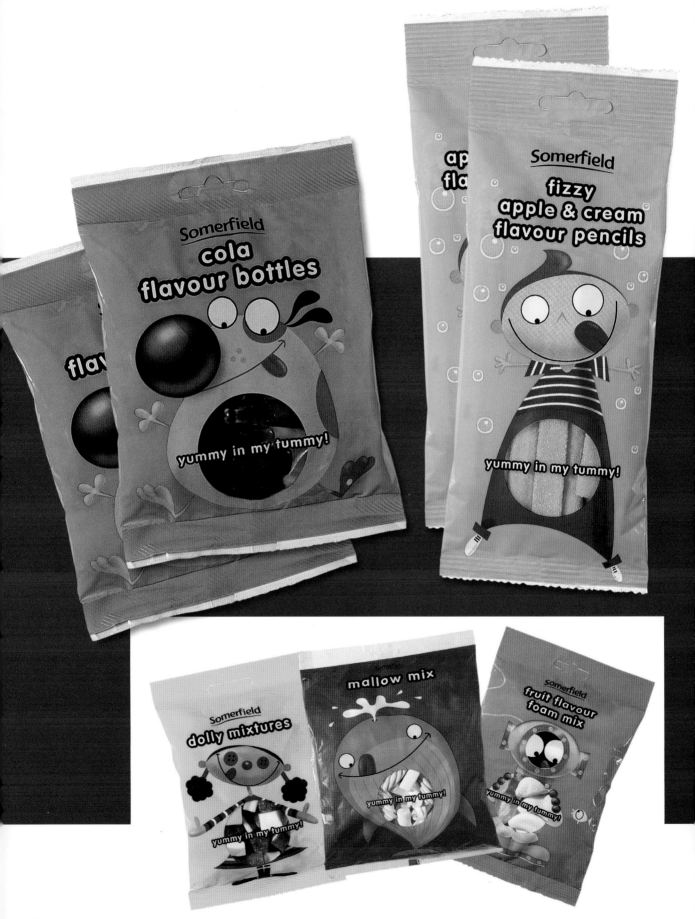

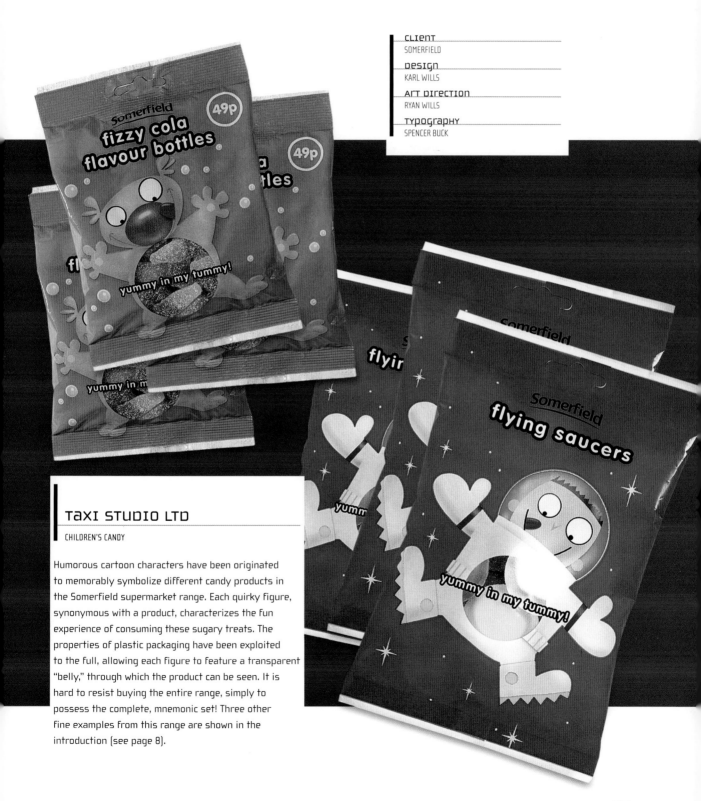

CLIENT
SOMERFIELD

DESIGN
KARL WILLS

ART DIRECTION
RYAN WILLS

TYPOGRAPHY
SPENCER BUCK

TAXI STUDIO LTD

CHILDREN'S CANDY

Humorous cartoon characters have been originated to memorably symbolize different candy products in the Somerfield supermarket range. Each quirky figure, synonymous with a product, characterizes the fun experience of consuming these sugary treats. The properties of plastic packaging have been exploited to the full, allowing each figure to feature a transparent "belly," through which the product can be seen. It is hard to resist buying the entire range, simply to possess the complete, mnemonic set! Three other fine examples from this range are shown in the introduction (see page 8).

materials and processes

UNUSUAL AND UNEXPECTED MATERIALS AND PROCESSES ARE INCLINED TO ATTRACT ATTENTION, BUT, MOST SIGNIFICANTLY, THEY ARE ALSO LIKELY TO BE REMEMBERED. IT IS SIMPLE TO DESCRIBE A PIECE OF WORK THAT INVOLVES DISTINCTIVE PRODUCTION TECHNIQUES AND SURFACES; IT CAN BE REFERRED TO AS "THE BROCHURE WITH THE RUBBER COVER," OR "THE LEAFLET ON PAPER WITH A STICKY SURFACE," OR "THE MAGAZINE THAT USES CUTOUTS," AND THE DESCRIPTION INSTANTLY TRIGGERS A COMPREHENSIVE RECOLLECTION OF THE ENTIRE ITEM. IT MAY BE DEBATABLE AS TO HOW RELEVANT AND APPROPRIATE THE DESIGNER'S CHOICE NEEDS TO BE IN CONNECTION WITH THE SUBJECT IN ORDER FOR A DESIGN TO BE MEMORABLE; A BOOK WITH A RUBBER COVER THAT HAPPENS TO BE ABOUT RUBBER OR ITEMS MANUFACTURED IN RUBBER WILL PROBABLY BE RECALLED FOR ITS COVER AS WELL AS ITS CONTENT, WHEREAS A BOOK ON FLOWER ARRANGING, WHICH JUST HAPPENS TO HAVE A RUBBER COVER, WILL BE REMEMBERED MERELY FOR ITS COVER, WITH LITTLE OR NO RECOLLECTION OF ITS CONTENT. THERE IS EVEN A DANGER THAT UNUSUAL MATERIALS AND PROCESSES USED PURELY TO BE DIFFERENT AND TO ATTRACT ATTENTION, IGNORING ANY LOGIC OR RELEVANCE, CAN ELICIT NEGATIVE RESPONSES FROM AUDIENCES, AS THEY MAY FIND THEM UNCOMFORTABLE AND OFF-PUTTING.

SECTION
U3

INEVITABLY, MOST DESIGNS ARE COST-DRIVEN; THEY ARE LITHO-PRINTED, AND MADE OUT OF STANDARD STOCK THAT IS PRACTICAL AND EFFICIENT. AS A CONSEQUENCE, ANYTHING THAT DIFFERS FROM THIS NORM WILL PROBABLY BE REGARDED AS DISTINCTIVE AND MEMORABLE. A WIDE RANGE OF MATERIALS AND PROCESSES CAN BE USED AS SUBSTITUTES FOR PAPER AND LITHO PRODUCTIONS, AND EACH CAN CREATE A STRONG VISUAL MNEMONIC.

DISTINCTIVE PROCESSES AND MATERIALS HELP TO CREATE SUCCESSFUL MEMORY DEVICES BECAUSE THEY STIMULATE MULTIPLE SENSES. THEY ARE NOT ONLY VISUALLY ATTRACTIVE, BUT ALSO IRRESISTIBLE TO THE TOUCH, AND COMPEL THE DESIRE TO INTERACT AND EXPERIENCE MORE. FOR EXAMPLE, A BROCHURE THAT INVOLVES THE SELECTIVE USE OF CUTOUTS AND VARNISHES DEMANDS THAT THE READER OPEN UP, EXPLORE, AND INTERACT WITH ITS PAGES. THE EXAMPLES THAT ARE SHOWN WITHIN THIS SECTION ARE EXCELLENT SAMPLES OF STRONG MNEMONICS THAT ARE ACHIEVED THROUGH THE DIVERSE USE OF MATERIALS AND PROCESSES—FROM DIE-CUTS TO FOLDING, THROUGH THE UTILIZATION OF RUBBER, TO KNITTING, PLASTIC, AND LIQUID—SHARING THE SENSE OF WONDER AND EXCITEMENT TO BE EXPERIENCED WHEN INTERACTING WITH THESE DESIGNS.

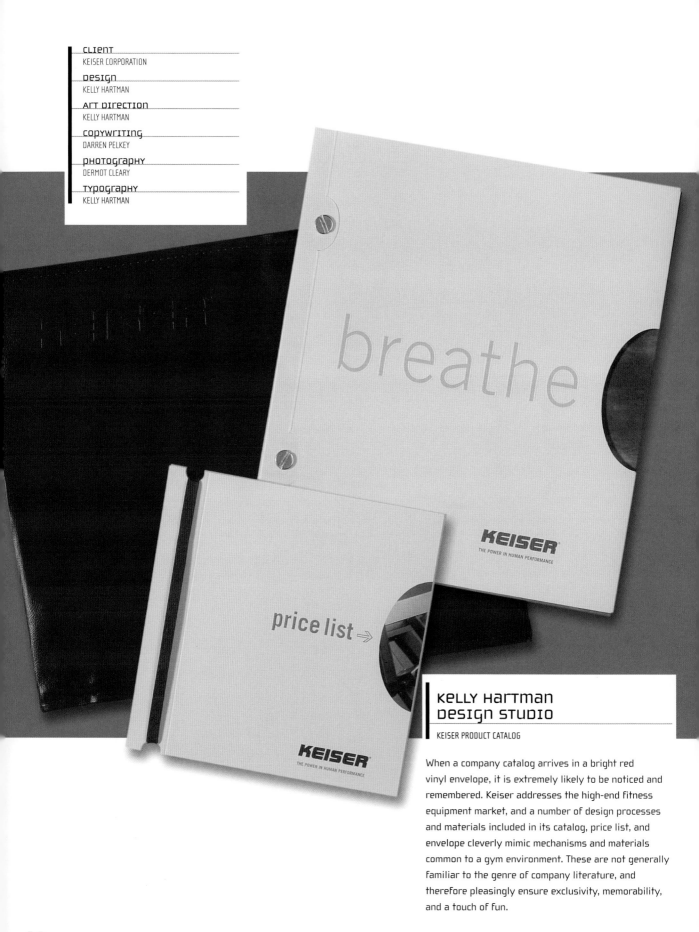

CLIENT
KEISER CORPORATION

DESIGN
KELLY HARTMAN

ART DIRECTION
KELLY HARTMAN

COPYWRITING
DARREN PELKEY

PHOTOGRAPHY
DERMOT CLEARY

TYPOGRAPHY
KELLY HARTMAN

KELLY HARTMAN DESIGN STUDIO

KEISER PRODUCT CATALOG

When a company catalog arrives in a bright red vinyl envelope, it is extremely likely to be noticed and remembered. Keiser addresses the high-end fitness equipment market, and a number of design processes and materials included in its catalog, price list, and envelope cleverly mimic mechanisms and materials common to a gym environment. These are not generally familiar to the genre of company literature, and therefore pleasingly ensure exclusivity, memorability, and a touch of fun.

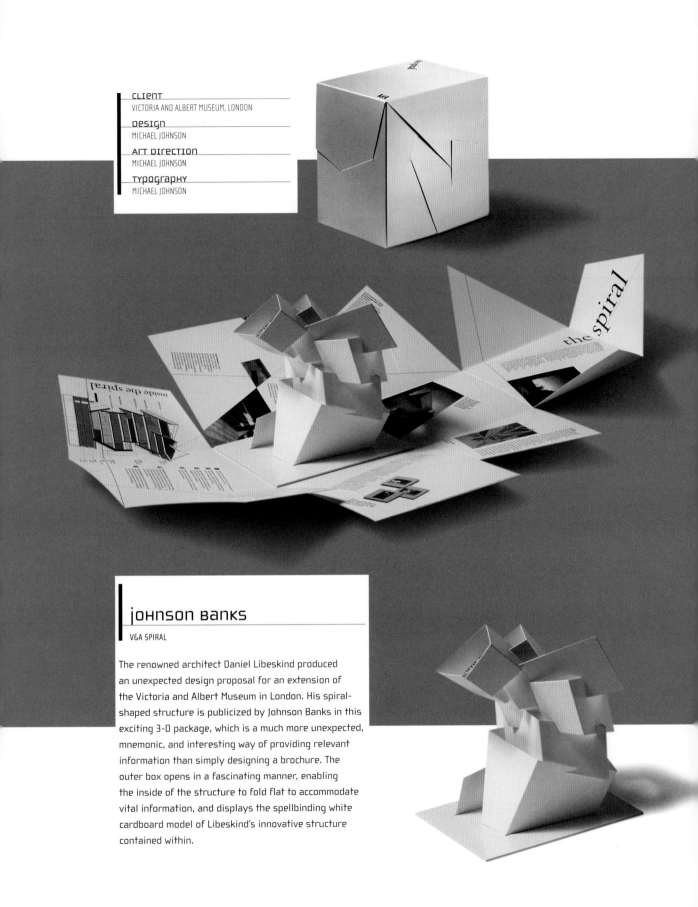

CLIENT
VICTORIA AND ALBERT MUSEUM, LONDON

DESIGN
MICHAEL JOHNSON

ART DIRECTION
MICHAEL JOHNSON

TYPOGRAPHY
MICHAEL JOHNSON

johnson banks

V&A SPIRAL

The renowned architect Daniel Libeskind produced
an unexpected design proposal for an extension of
the Victoria and Albert Museum in London. His spiral-
shaped structure is publicized by Johnson Banks in this
exciting 3-D package, which is a much more unexpected,
mnemonic, and interesting way of providing relevant
information than simply designing a brochure. The
outer box opens in a fascinating manner, enabling
the inside of the structure to fold flat to accommodate
vital information, and displays the spellbinding white
cardboard model of Libeskind's innovative structure
contained within.

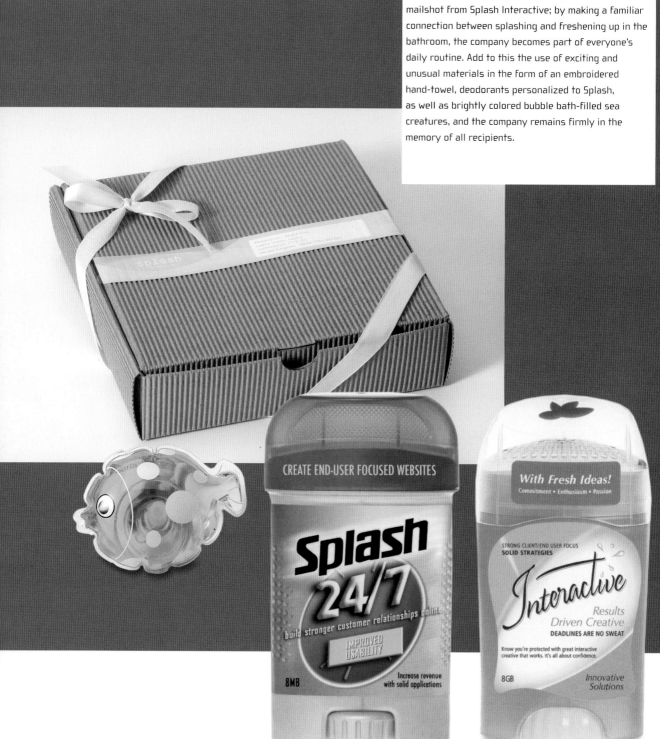

SPLASH INTERACTIVE

"FRESHEN UP AND REVITALIZE" SELF-PROMOTION

It would be hard to forget this self-promotional mailshot from Splash Interactive; by making a familiar connection between splashing and freshening up in the bathroom, the company becomes part of everyone's daily routine. Add to this the use of exciting and unusual materials in the form of an embroidered hand-towel, deodorants personalized to Splash, as well as brightly colored bubble bath-filled sea creatures, and the company remains firmly in the memory of all recipients.

CREATE END-USER FOCUSED WEBSITES

Splash
24/7

build stronger customer relationships online

IMPROVED
USABILITY

8MB

Increase revenue
with solid applications

With Fresh Ideas!
Commitment • Enthusiasm • Passion

STRONG CLIENT/END USER FOCUS
SOLID STRATEGIES

Interactive

Results
Driven Creative
DEADLINES ARE NO SWEAT

Know you're protected with great interactive
creative that works. It's all about confidence.

8GB

Innovative
Solutions

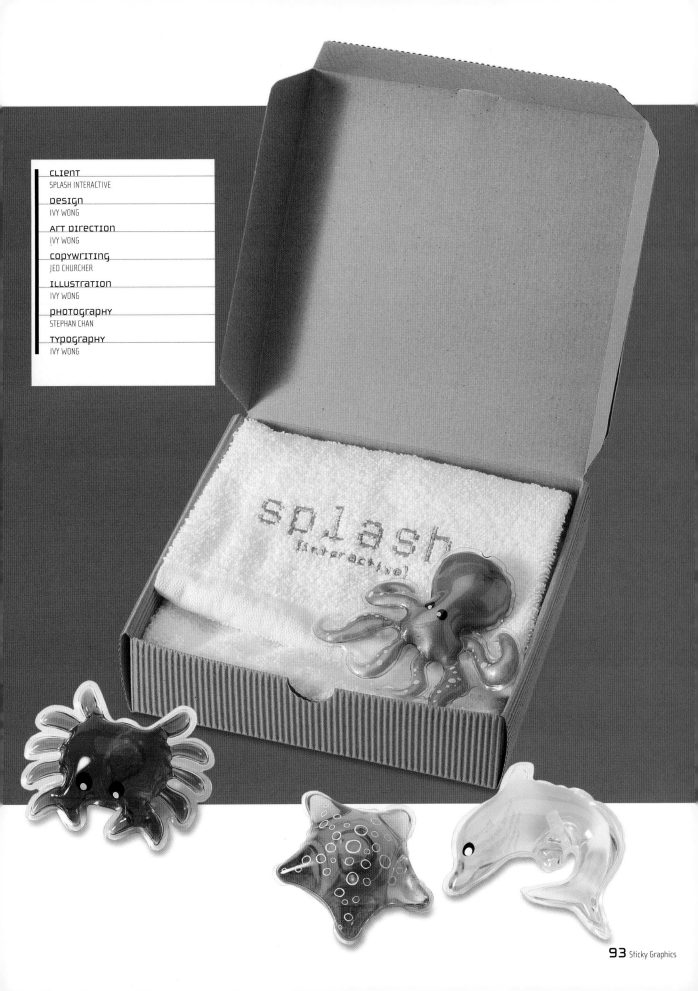

CLIENT
SPLASH INTERACTIVE

DESIGN
IVY WONG

ART DIRECTION
IVY WONG

COPYWRITING
JED CHURCHER

ILLUSTRATION
IVY WONG

PHOTOGRAPHY
STEPHAN CHAN

TYPOGRAPHY
IVY WONG

FRANCESCA

A FILM BY ALEXIS RUSSO

CLIENT
ALEXIS RUSSO
DESIGN
CHRIS RUBINO
ART DIRECTION
CHRIS RUBINO
ILLUSTRATION
CHRIS RUBINO

CHRIS RUBINO

FILM POSTER

This striking silkscreened poster for *Francesca*, a film by Alexis Russo, is memorable for two reasons: first, the central positioning of Francesca's portrait, which appears almost in silhouette, and second, Chris Rubino's subtle and surprising use of varnish to print all facial features. "The film is about dementia," explains Chris. "Printing the woman's face in clear varnish gave the image a fading effect, symbolic of the disease." The image is particularly unforgettable because it elicits an empathetic response from the viewer contemplating the tragic consequences of this condition.

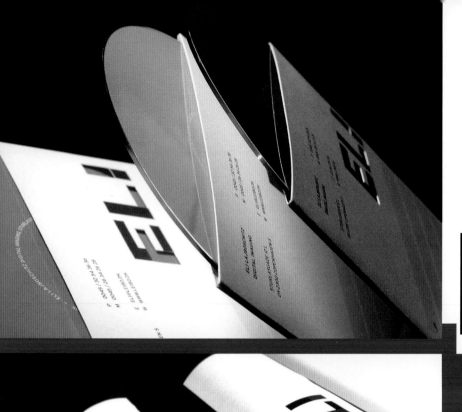

CLIENT
ELI DIGITAL IMAGING

DESIGN
MUGGIE RAMADANI AND CLAUS RYSSER

ART DIRECTION
MUGGIE RAMADANI

TYPOGRAPHY
MUGGIE RAMADANI

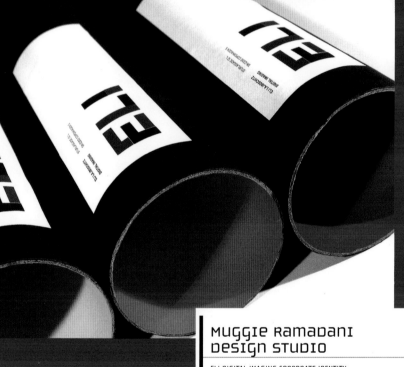

MUGGIE RAMADANI DESIGN STUDIO

ELI DIGITAL IMAGING CORPORATE IDENTITY

The visually exciting impact of black, white, and gray contrasting with hot red, orange, and yellow provides this corporate identity from Muggie Ramadani with enduring qualities that make it stand out from the crowd. However, the realization that the first glimpse of vibrant color is through cutout windows incorporated in the letters making "ELI," undoubtedly gives the design its lasting presence. CD covers, stationery, and packing tubes are all monochrome black and white on the outside, and the windows expose a tempting taste of the color to come.

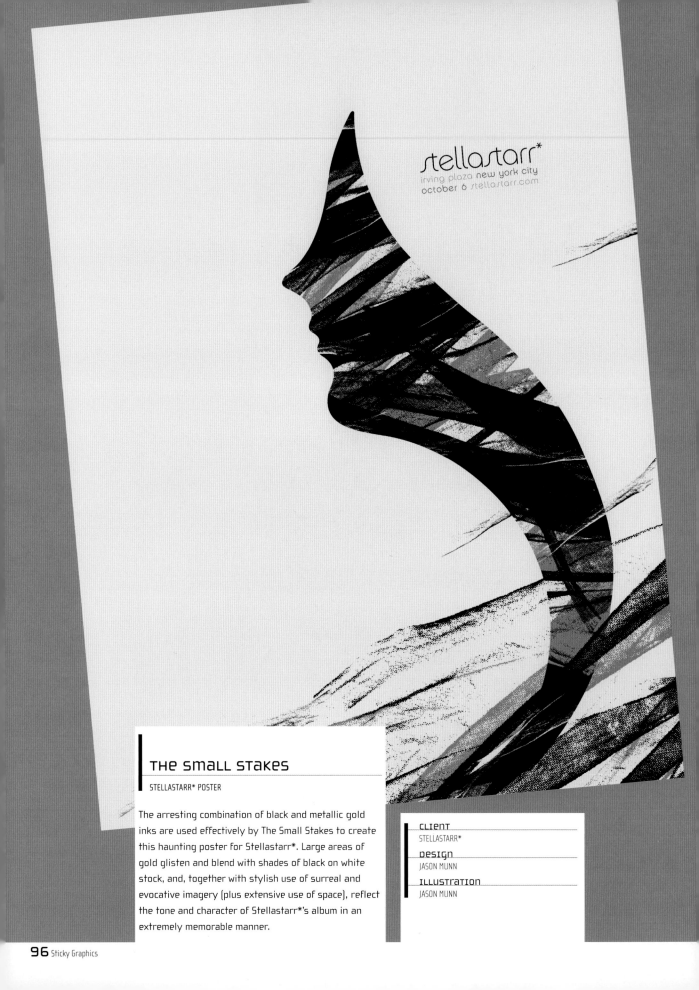

stellastarr*
irving plaza new york city
october 6 stellastarr.com

THE SMALL STAKES

STELLASTARR* POSTER

The arresting combination of black and metallic gold
inks are used effectively by The Small Stakes to create
this haunting poster for Stellastarr*. Large areas of
gold glisten and blend with shades of black on white
stock, and, together with stylish use of surreal and
evocative imagery (plus extensive use of space), reflect
the tone and character of Stellastarr*'s album in an
extremely memorable manner.

CLIENT
STELLASTARR*
DESIGN
JASON MUNN
ILLUSTRATION
JASON MUNN

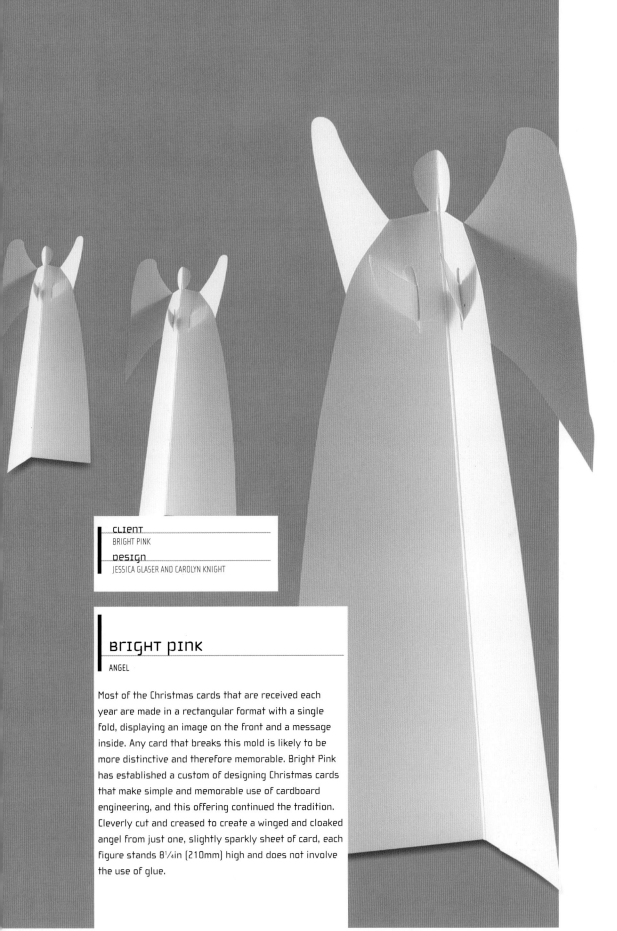

CLIENT
BRIGHT PINK

DESIGN
JESSICA GLASER AND CAROLYN KNIGHT

BRIGHT PINK

ANGEL

Most of the Christmas cards that are received each year are made in a rectangular format with a single fold, displaying an image on the front and a message inside. Any card that breaks this mold is likely to be more distinctive and therefore memorable. Bright Pink has established a custom of designing Christmas cards that make simple and memorable use of cardboard engineering, and this offering continued the tradition. Cleverly cut and creased to create a winged and cloaked angel from just one, slightly sparkly sheet of card, each figure stands 8¼in (210mm) high and does not involve the use of glue.

snap-e-chuck inc.

SNAP-E-CHUCK INC. BUSINESS CARD

The truly innovative and considered implementation of clear rigid plastic as the stock for these business cards makes them mnemonic. The combination of fluorescent pink, bright blue, black, and white in the design makes the cards very eye-catching; however, it is the carefully selected see-through areas of a star in the bottom left corner, and the smoke from a gun, that create the intriguing, ever-changing format of the cards as they pass over different surfaces.

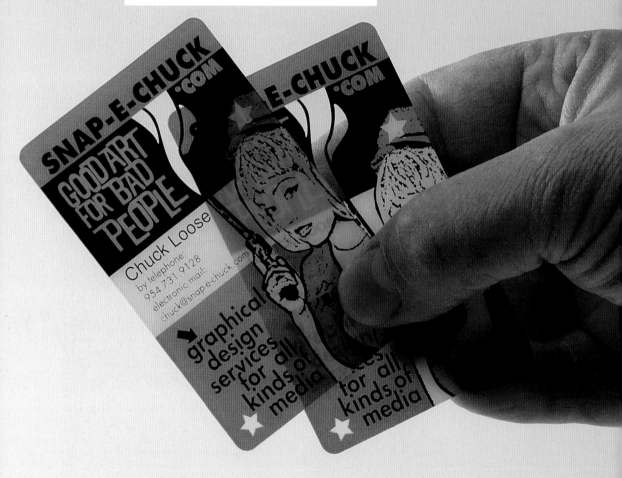

CLIENT
SNAP-E-CHUCK INC.

DESIGN
CHUCK LOOSE

ILLUSTRATION
CHUCK LOOSE

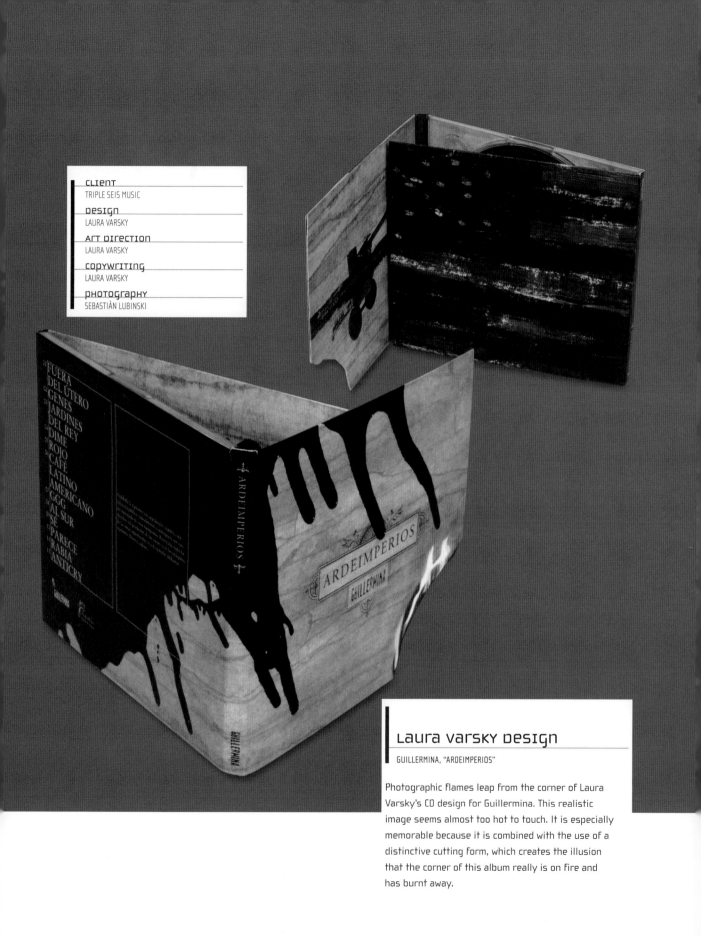

CLIENT
TRIPLE SEIS MUSIC

DESIGN
LAURA VARSKY

ART DIRECTION
LAURA VARSKY

COPYWRITING
LAURA VARSKY

PHOTOGRAPHY
SEBASTIÀN LUBINSKI

LAURA VARSKY DESIGN

GUILLERMINA, "ARDEIMPERIOS"

Photographic flames leap from the corner of Laura Varsky's CD design for Guillermina. This realistic image seems almost too hot to touch. It is especially memorable because it is combined with the use of a distinctive cutting form, which creates the illusion that the corner of this album really is on fire and has burnt away.

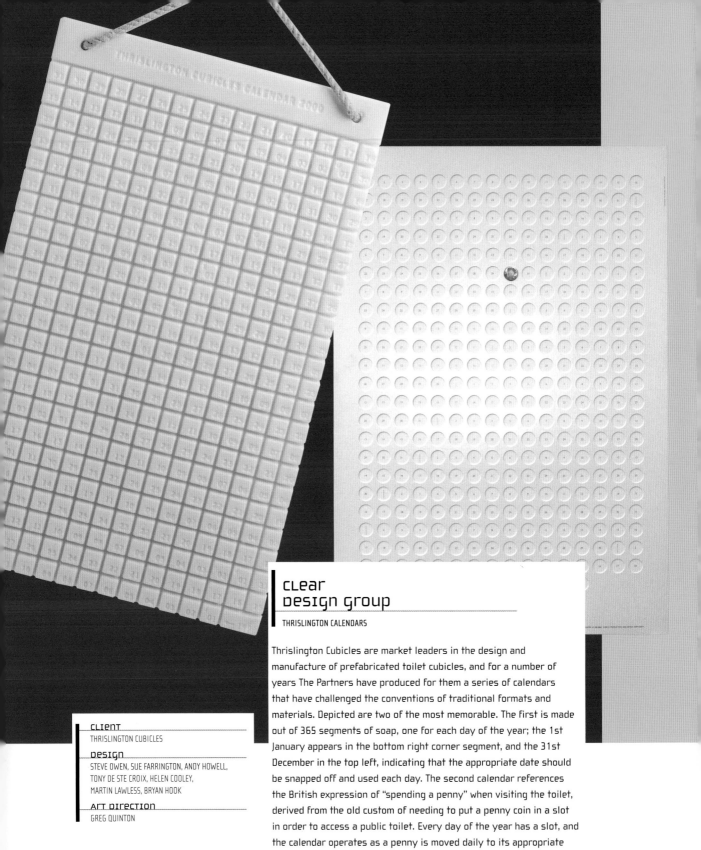

cLear
Desıgn group

THRISLINGTON CALENDARS

Thrislington Cubicles are market leaders in the design and manufacture of prefabricated toilet cubicles, and for a number of years The Partners have produced for them a series of calendars that have challenged the conventions of traditional formats and materials. Depicted are two of the most memorable. The first is made out of 365 segments of soap, one for each day of the year; the 1st January appears in the bottom right corner segment, and the 31st December in the top left, indicating that the appropriate date should be snapped off and used each day. The second calendar references the British expression of "spending a penny" when visiting the toilet, derived from the old custom of needing to put a penny coin in a slot in order to access a public toilet. Every day of the year has a slot, and the calendar operates as a penny is moved daily to its appropriate position. Both concepts trigger a combination of amusement and intrigue, but become particularly enduring and memorable because they are constructed in the correct materials, and actually function.

CLIENT
THRISLINGTON CUBICLES

DESIGN
STEVE OWEN, SUE FARRINGTON, ANDY HOWELL,
TONY DE STE CROIX, HELEN COOLEY,
MARTIN LAWLESS, BRYAN HOOK

Art Direction
GREG QUINTON

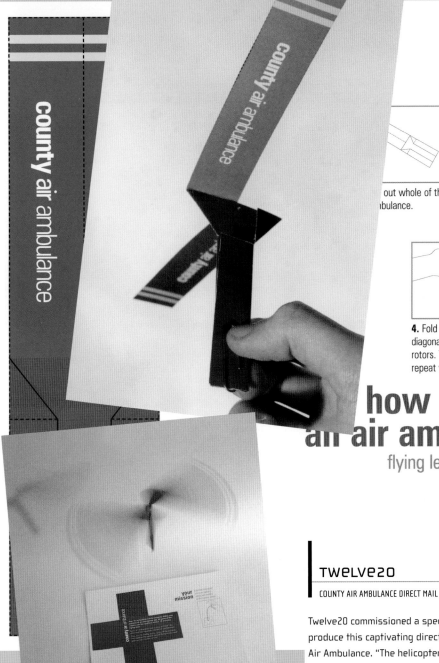

Cut along the dotted lines to form an air ambulance and follow instructions.

out whole of the ...bulance.

2. Cut along all of the dotted lines on rotor blades and body.

3. Fold bo... the solid lir... the centre.

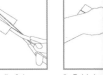
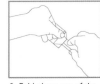
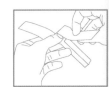

4. Fold along one of the diagonal lines towards rotors. Turn over and repeat with other one.

5. Fold one of the rotor blades down towards the body. Turn over and do same to the other.

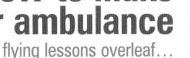

how to make an air ambulance
flying lessons overleaf…

7. You shou... your comp... ambulance

TWELVE20

COUNTY AIR AMBULANCE DIRECT MAIL

Twelve20 commissioned a special cutting form to produce this captivating direct-mail design for County Air Ambulance. "The helicopter is an interactive piece, which takes the viewer back to recollections of childhood," says designer Darren Langham. "Through being involved in the making and then playing with the helicopter, it enables the viewer to have fun, remember the charity, and hopefully donate plenty of money."

CLIENT
COUNTY AIR AMBULANCE

DESIGN
DARREN LANGHAM AND MATTHEW TULLETT

ART DIRECTION
DARREN LANGHAM AND MATTHEW TULLETT

COPYWRITING
DARREN LANGHAM AND PAUL WEIR

ILLUSTRATION
DARREN LANGHAM

THames & HUDSON

RUBBER: FUN FASHION FETISH

Designed by Henrik Langsdorf for Thames & Hudson, *Rubber: Fun Fashion Fetish* is guaranteed to provide an amusing and lasting impression, as it features a bright orange, flexible, molded rubber cover. Not only does this serve as an excellent visual mnemonic, but it also demands to be touched. The experience of sensing a soft and springy textured material around a book is so unusual that it is unforgettable.

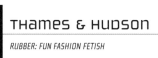

CLIENT
THAMES & HUDSON

DESIGN
HENRIK LANGSDORF

ART DIRECTION
HENRIK LANGSDORF

ILLUSTRATION
OTTO STEINBERGER

TYPOGRAPHY
HENRIK LANGSDORF

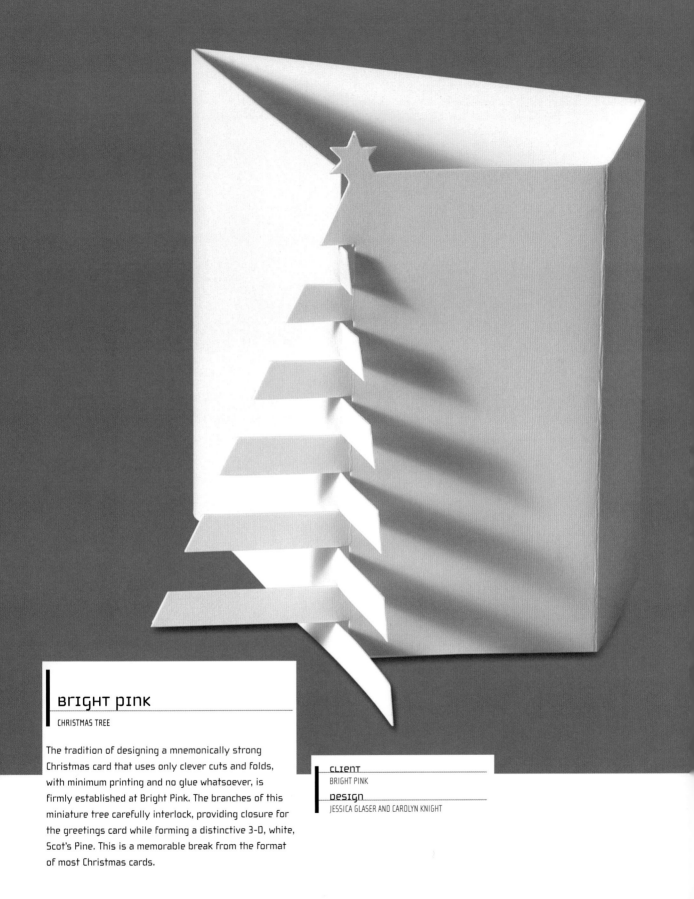

BriGHT PiNK

CHRISTMAS TREE

The tradition of designing a mnemonically strong
Christmas card that uses only clever cuts and folds,
with minimum printing and no glue whatsoever, is
firmly established at Bright Pink. The branches of this
miniature tree carefully interlock, providing closure for
the greetings card while forming a distinctive 3-D, white,
Scot's Pine. This is a memorable break from the format
of most Christmas cards.

CLIENT
BRIGHT PINK

DESIGN
JESSICA GLASER AND CAROLYN KNIGHT

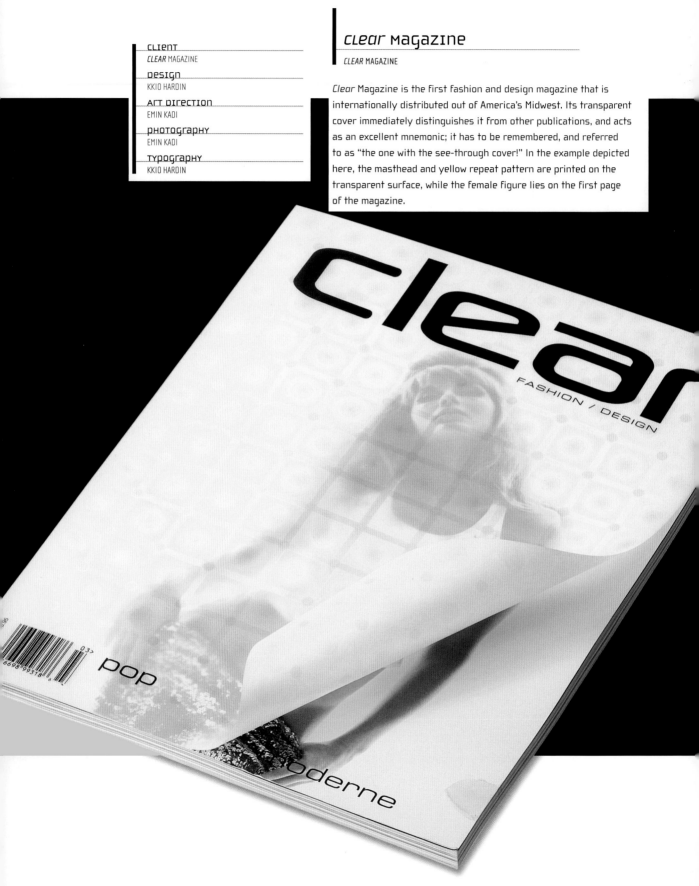

CLIENT
CLEAR MAGAZINE

DESIGN
KKID HARDIN

ART DIRECTION
EMIN KADI

PHOTOGRAPHY
EMIN KADI

TYPOGRAPHY
KKID HARDIN

CLEAR MAGAZINE
CLEAR MAGAZINE

Clear Magazine is the first fashion and design magazine that is internationally distributed out of America's Midwest. Its transparent cover immediately distinguishes it from other publications, and acts as an excellent mnemonic; it has to be remembered, and referred to as "the one with the see-through cover!" In the example depicted here, the masthead and yellow repeat pattern are printed on the transparent surface, while the female figure lies on the first page of the magazine.

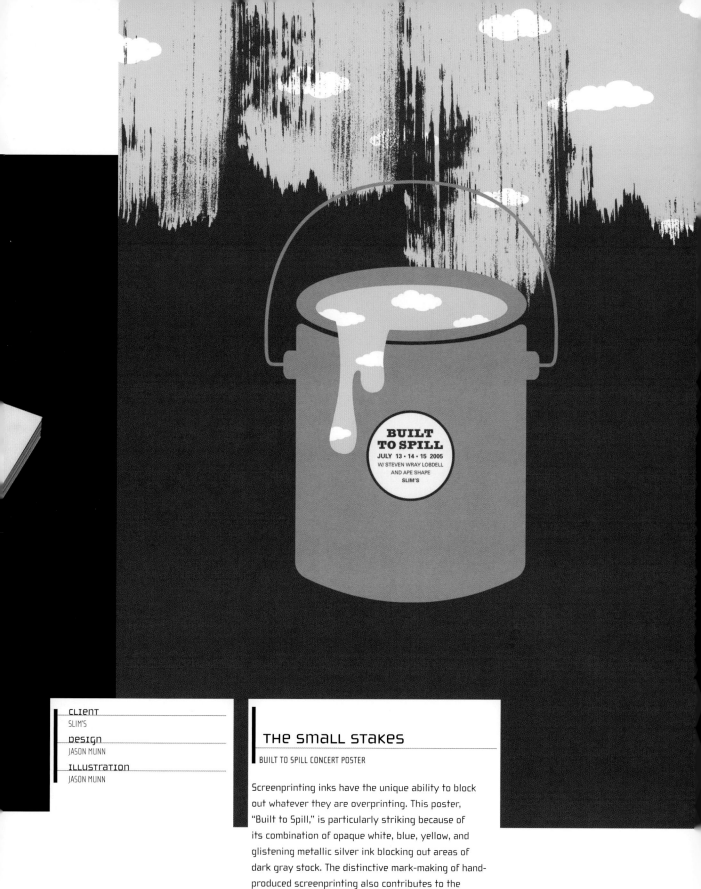

CLIENT
SLIM'S

DESIGN
JASON MUNN

ILLUSTRATION
JASON MUNN

THE SMALL STAKES

BUILT TO SPILL CONCERT POSTER

Screenprinting inks have the unique ability to block out whatever they are overprinting. This poster, "Built to Spill," is particularly striking because of its combination of opaque white, blue, yellow, and glistening metallic silver ink blocking out areas of dark gray stock. The distinctive mark-making of hand-produced screenprinting also contributes to the poster's appeal and lasting impression.

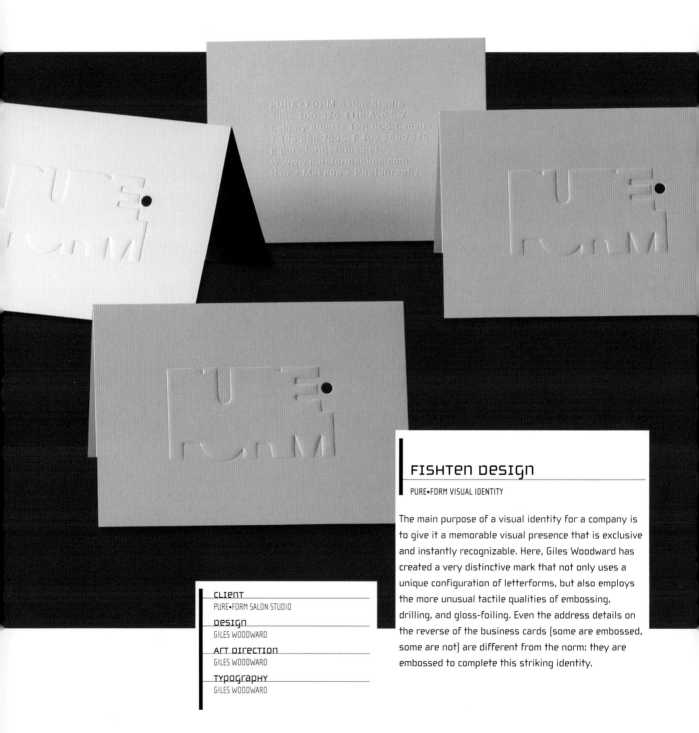

FISHTEN DESIGN

PURE•FORM VISUAL IDENTITY

The main purpose of a visual identity for a company is to give it a memorable visual presence that is exclusive and instantly recognizable. Here, Giles Woodward has created a very distinctive mark that not only uses a unique configuration of letterforms, but also employs the more unusual tactile qualities of embossing, drilling, and gloss-foiling. Even the address details on the reverse of the business cards (some are embossed, some are not) are different from the norm: they are embossed to complete this striking identity.

CLIENT
PURE•FORM SALON STUDIO

DESIGN
GILES WOODWARD

ART DIRECTION
GILES WOODWARD

TYPOGRAPHY
GILES WOODWARD

BankerWessel

ARKITEKTUR 1 SVERIGE

Architecture is about the design and construction of buildings, and the inspirational cover of this book on architecture is dominated by a brightly colored die-cut that punches out, folds, and fastens in the form of a cardboard house. The concept is memorable because it differs from most book covers; if recipients actually make their own house, the 3-D model becomes a constant reminder and iconic representation of this BankerWessel client.

CLIENT
ARKITEKTURMUSEET

DESIGN
IDA WESSEL

ART DIRECTION
IDA WESSEL

COPYWRITING
DAVID POWELL AND SUSSANNA JANFALK

ILLUSTRATION
JONAS BANKER

TYPOGRAPHY
IDA WESSEL

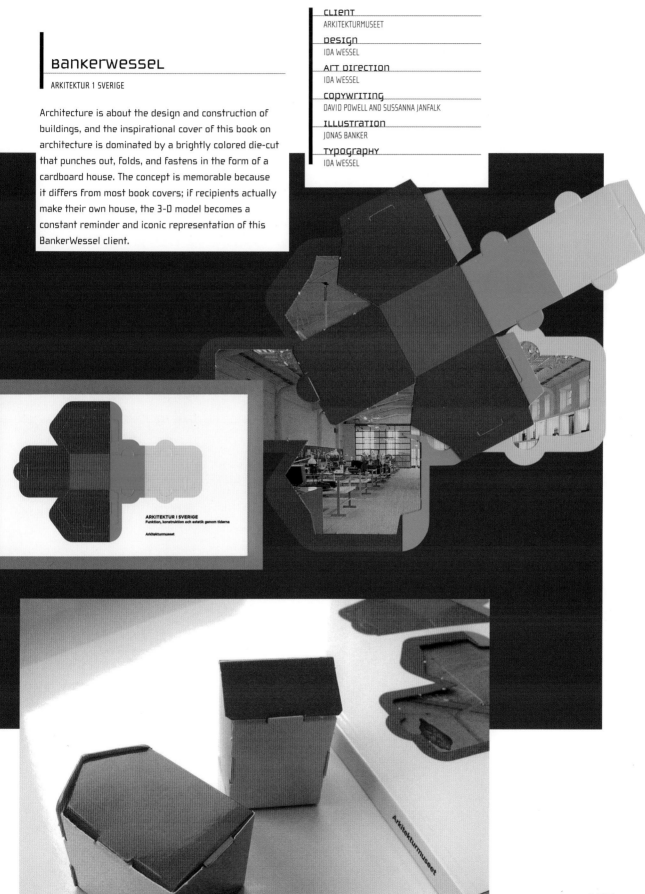

ARKITEKTUR I SVERIGE
Funktion, konstruktion och estetik genom tiderna

Arkitekturmuseet

Arkitekturmuseet

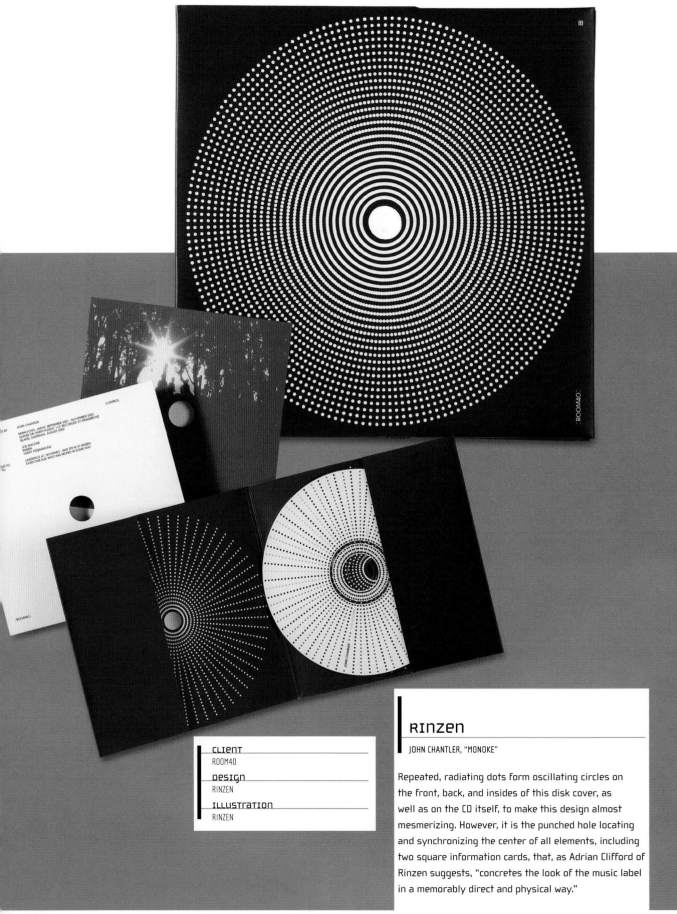

RINZEN

JOHN CHANTLER, "MONOKE"

Repeated, radiating dots form oscillating circles on the front, back, and insides of this disk cover, as well as on the CD itself, to make this design almost mesmerizing. However, it is the punched hole locating and synchronizing the center of all elements, including two square information cards, that, as Adrian Clifford of Rinzen suggests, "concretes the look of the music label in a memorably direct and physical way."

CLIENT
ROOM40

DESIGN
RINZEN

ILLUSTRATION
RINZEN

Minimum Finger Length 14cm.
Net Weight 28 lb (12.7Kg)

Product of

Belize

CLIENT
BIRMINGHAM ARTS TRUST
DESIGN
JEFF LEAK AND GILES WOODWARD
ART DIRECTION
JEFF LEAK AND GILES WOODWARD
PHOTOGRAPHY
JEFF LEAK
TYPOGRAPHY
JEFF LEAK AND GILES WOODWARD

DISPLAY
SWEET LIFE

LIMITED EDITION 68 / 200

BAT (0121) 643 6040

1. PASSPORT TO A HAPPY STATE
2. WORK OF A FRIVOLOUS NATURE
3. YARDSTICK
4. SEEDLESS

ANGELINA MAY DAVIS,
KEITH PEARSALL

MICK THACKER, MARK RENN

LEE WILLIAMS, KIM MERRINGTON,
PETER DENSON, SIMON BROOME,
E WITCOMB, TOM RANAHAN,

CAROLYN MORTON,
ANNE-MARIE COPESTAKE
ALISTAIR SCRUTON, REID SMITH
ANGELINA MAY DAVIS,
KEITH PEARSALL, ANA RUTTER

BOING!

SWEET LIFE

"This limited-edition artists' catalog has proven to be
an extremely sought-after and memorable giveaway,"
says Jeff Leak of Boing! The piece was inspired by the
idea of the artist as "sweet fruit" being packaged and
sold, with each cover actually cut from discarded fruit
cartons, and bolted to the internal pages of the catalog.
Titling labels are affixed to the front, in the same
manner as they would be to a box of fruit. Just to add
to the memorable nature of this design—but only for
those with a handy scanner—the bar code reads:
"Sweet Life."

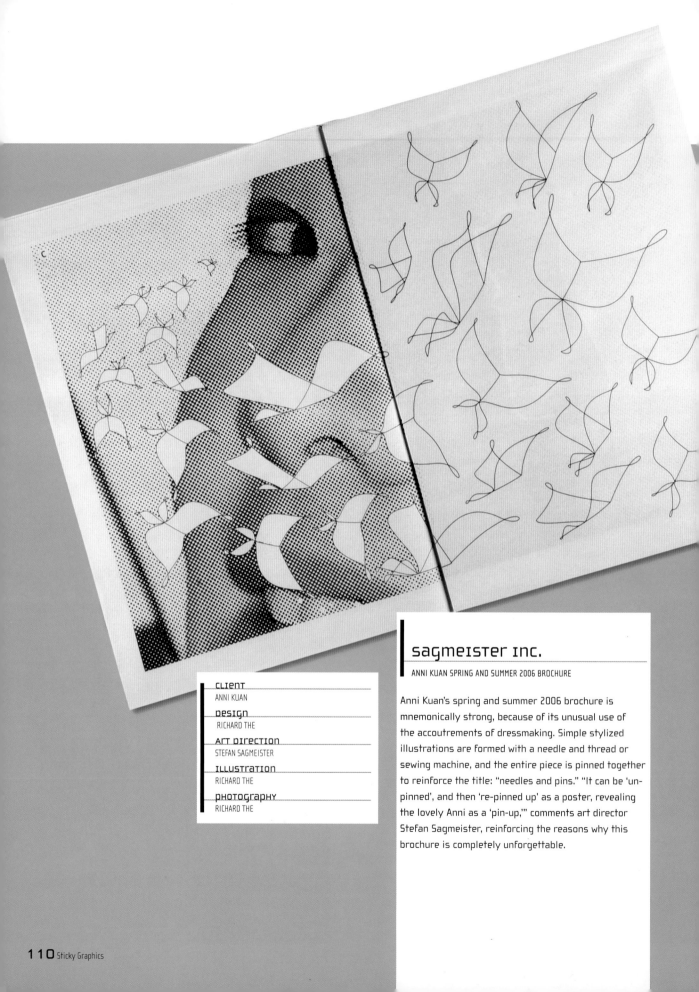

sagmeister inc.

Anni Kuan's spring and summer 2006 brochure is mnemonically strong, because of its unusual use of the accoutrements of dressmaking. Simple stylized illustrations are formed with a needle and thread or sewing machine, and the entire piece is pinned together to reinforce the title: "needles and pins." "It can be 'un-pinned', and then 're-pinned up' as a poster, revealing the lovely Anni as a 'pin-up,'" comments art director Stefan Sagmeister, reinforcing the reasons why this brochure is completely unforgettable.

CLIENT
ANNI KUAN

DESIGN
RICHARD THE

ART DIRECTION
STEFAN SAGMEISTER

ILLUSTRATION
RICHARD THE

PHOTOGRAPHY
RICHARD THE

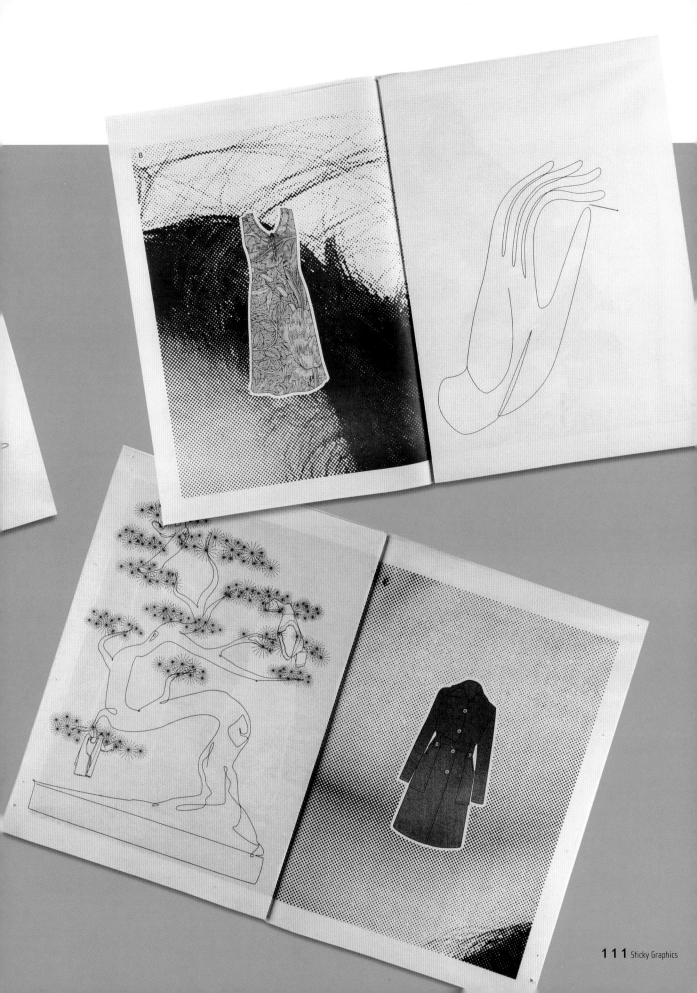

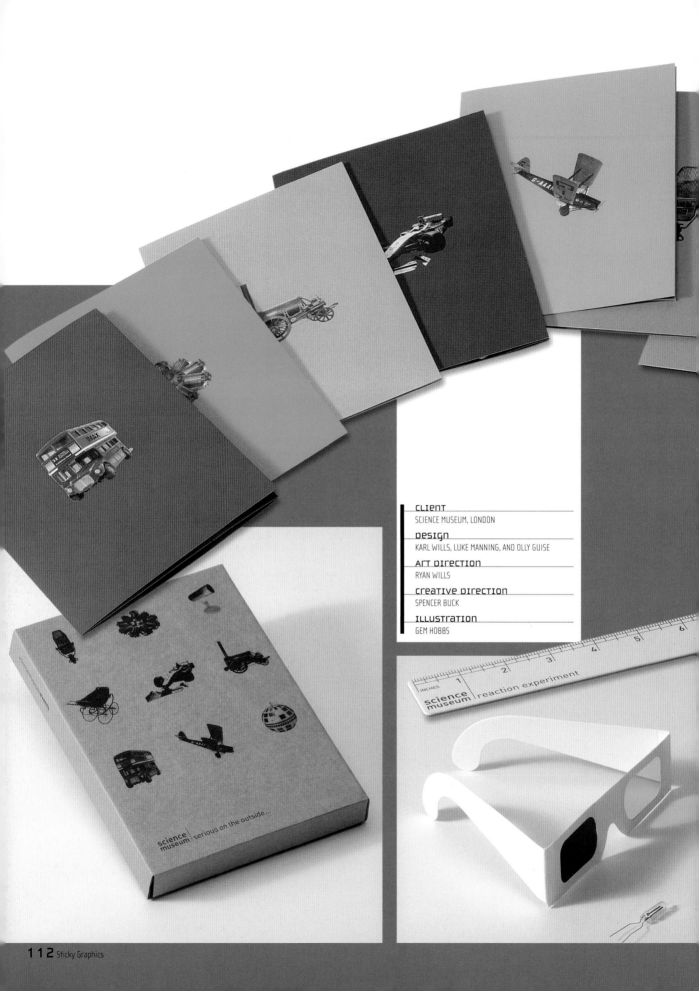

CLIENT
SCIENCE MUSEUM, LONDON

DESIGN
KARL WILLS, LUKE MANNING, AND OLLY GUISE

ART DIRECTION
RYAN WILLS

CREATIVE DIRECTION
SPENCER BUCK

ILLUSTRATION
GEM HOBBS

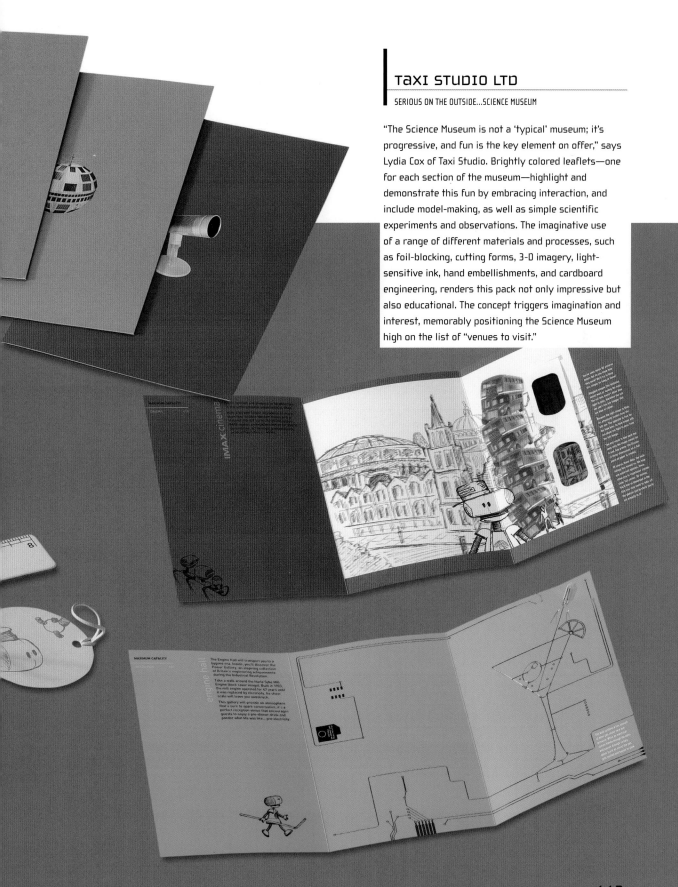

TAXI STUDIO LTD

SERIOUS ON THE OUTSIDE...SCIENCE MUSEUM

"The Science Museum is not a 'typical' museum; it's progressive, and fun is the key element on offer," says Lydia Cox of Taxi Studio. Brightly colored leaflets—one for each section of the museum—highlight and demonstrate this fun by embracing interaction, and include model-making, as well as simple scientific experiments and observations. The imaginative use of a range of different materials and processes, such as foil-blocking, cutting forms, 3-D imagery, light-sensitive ink, hand embellishments, and cardboard engineering, renders this pack not only impressive but also educational. The concept triggers imagination and interest, memorably positioning the Science Museum high on the list of "venues to visit."

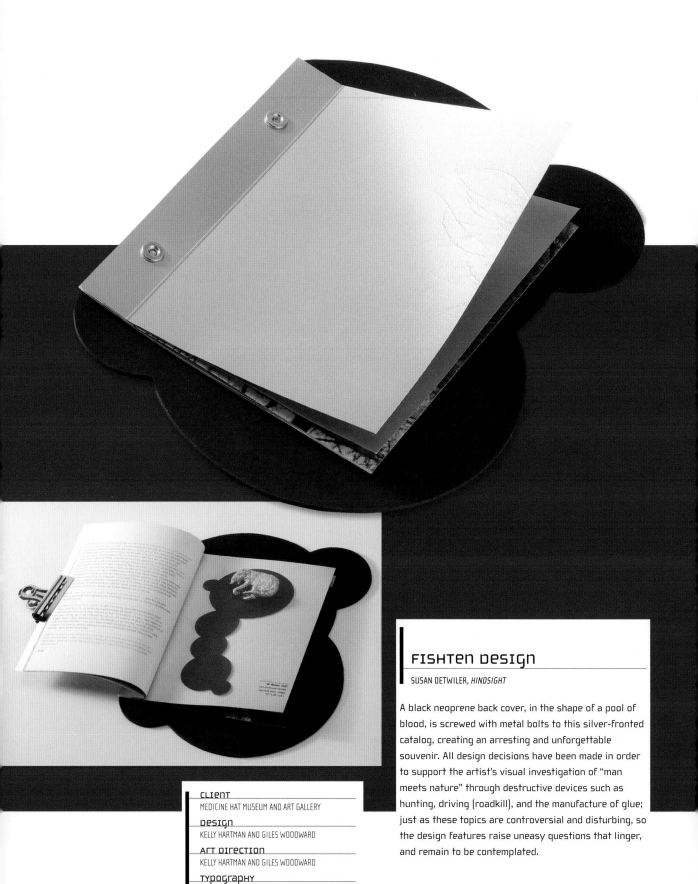

FISHTEN DESIGN

SUSAN DETWILER, *HINDSIGHT*

A black neoprene back cover, in the shape of a pool of blood, is screwed with metal bolts to this silver-fronted catalog, creating an arresting and unforgettable souvenir. All design decisions have been made in order to support the artist's visual investigation of "man meets nature" through destructive devices such as hunting, driving (roadkill), and the manufacture of glue; just as these topics are controversial and disturbing, so the design features raise uneasy questions that linger, and remain to be contemplated.

CLIENT
MEDICINE HAT MUSEUM AND ART GALLERY

DESIGN
KELLY HARTMAN AND GILES WOODWARD

ART DIRECTION
KELLY HARTMAN AND GILES WOODWARD

TYPOGRAPHY
KELLY HARTMAN AND GILES WOODWARD

COPYWRITING
SUSEI MAJOR

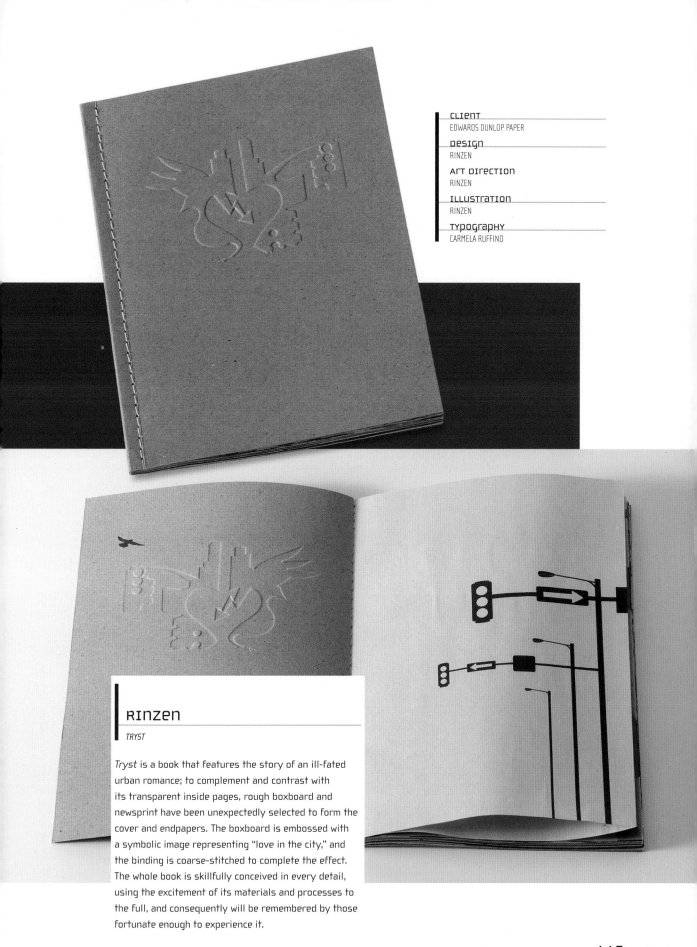

CLIENT
EDWARDS DUNLOP PAPER

DESIGN
RINZEN

ART DIRECTION
RINZEN

ILLUSTRATION
RINZEN

TYPOGRAPHY
CARMELA RUFFINO

RINZEN

TRYST

Tryst is a book that features the story of an ill-fated urban romance; to complement and contrast with its transparent inside pages, rough boxboard and newsprint have been unexpectedly selected to form the cover and endpapers. The boxboard is embossed with a symbolic image representing "love in the city," and the binding is coarse-stitched to complete the effect. The whole book is skillfully conceived in every detail, using the excitement of its materials and processes to the full, and consequently will be remembered by those fortunate enough to experience it.

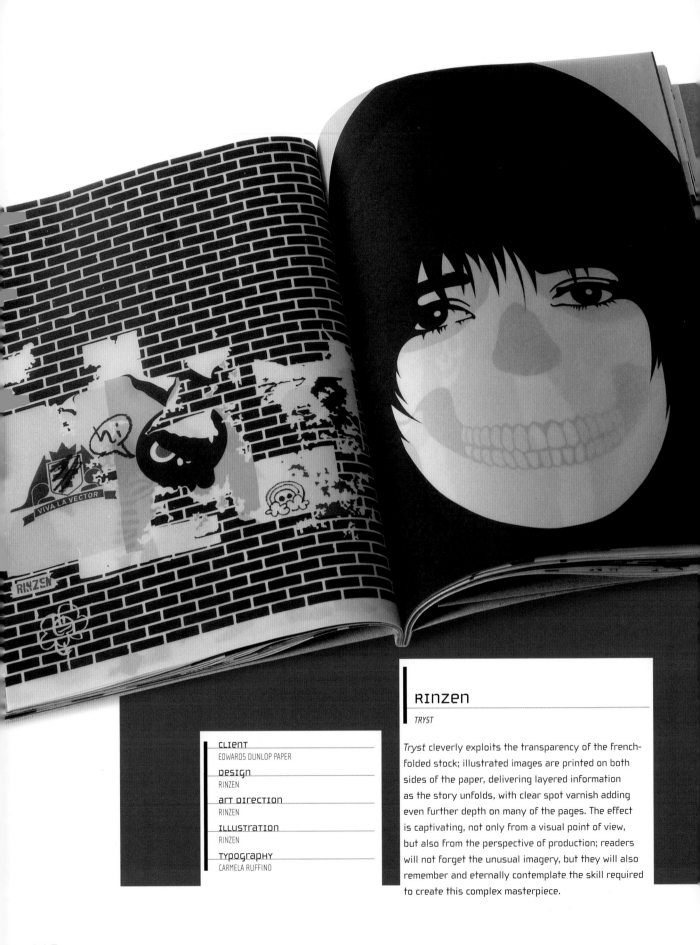

RINZEN

TRYST

Tryst cleverly exploits the transparency of the french-folded stock; illustrated images are printed on both sides of the paper, delivering layered information as the story unfolds, with clear spot varnish adding even further depth on many of the pages. The effect is captivating, not only from a visual point of view, but also from the perspective of production; readers will not forget the unusual imagery, but they will also remember and eternally contemplate the skill required to create this complex masterpiece.

CLIENT
EDWARDS DUNLOP PAPER

DESIGN
RINZEN

ART DIRECTION
RINZEN

ILLUSTRATION
RINZEN

TYPOGRAPHY
CARMELA RUFFINO

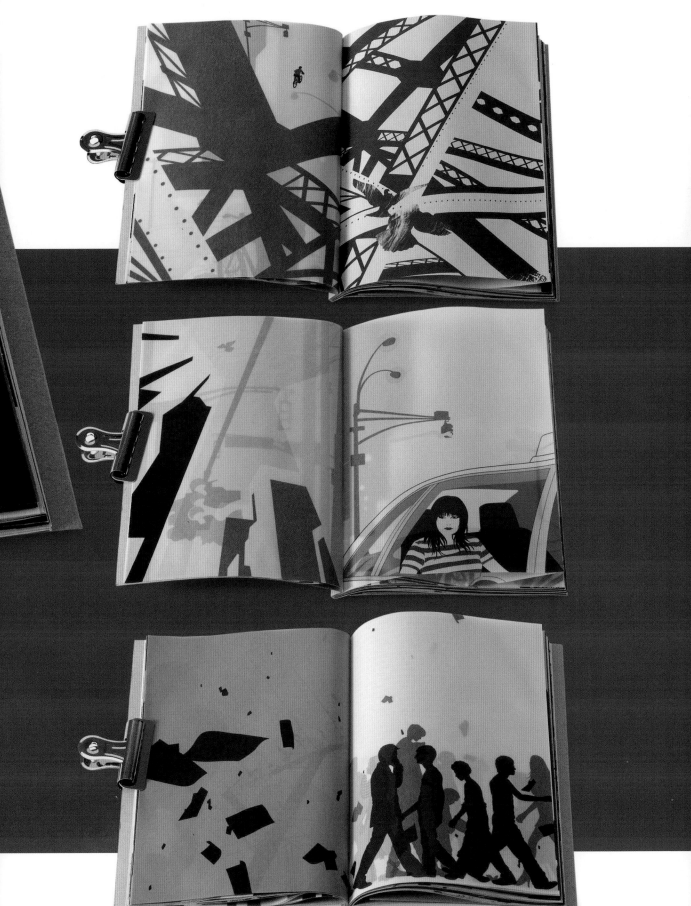

CLIENT
PUBLIC ART COMMISSIONS AGENCY

DESIGN
JEFF LEAK AND GILES WOODWARD

ART DIRECTION
JEFF LEAK AND GILES WOODWARD

PHOTOGRAPHY
JEFF LEAK

TYPOGRAPHY
JEFF LEAK AND GILES WOODWARD

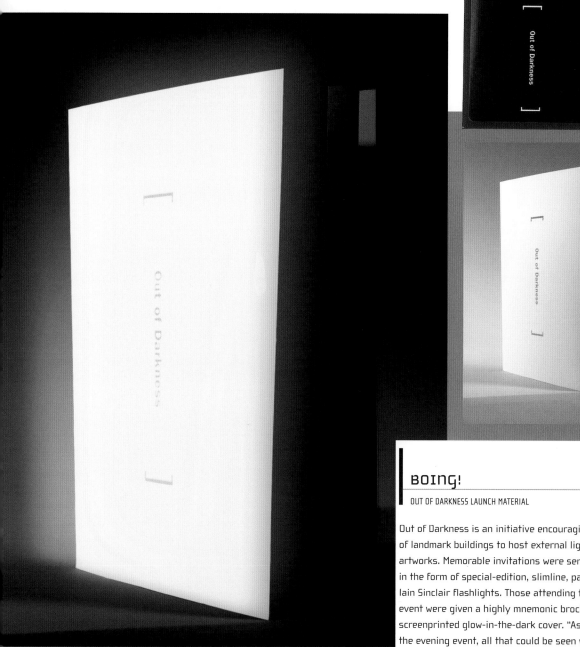

BOING!

OUT OF DARKNESS LAUNCH MATERIAL

Out of Darkness is an initiative encouraging owners of landmark buildings to host external light-based artworks. Memorable invitations were sent out in the form of special-edition, slimline, paper-covered Iain Sinclair flashlights. Those attending the launch event were given a highly mnemonic brochure, with a screenprinted glow-in-the-dark cover. "As people left the evening event, all that could be seen were the luminous brochures moving up and down the road," comments Jeff Leak of Boing! The fascinating properties of this launch material ensured that it would be kept by recipients, as a highly memorable and interactive souvenir.

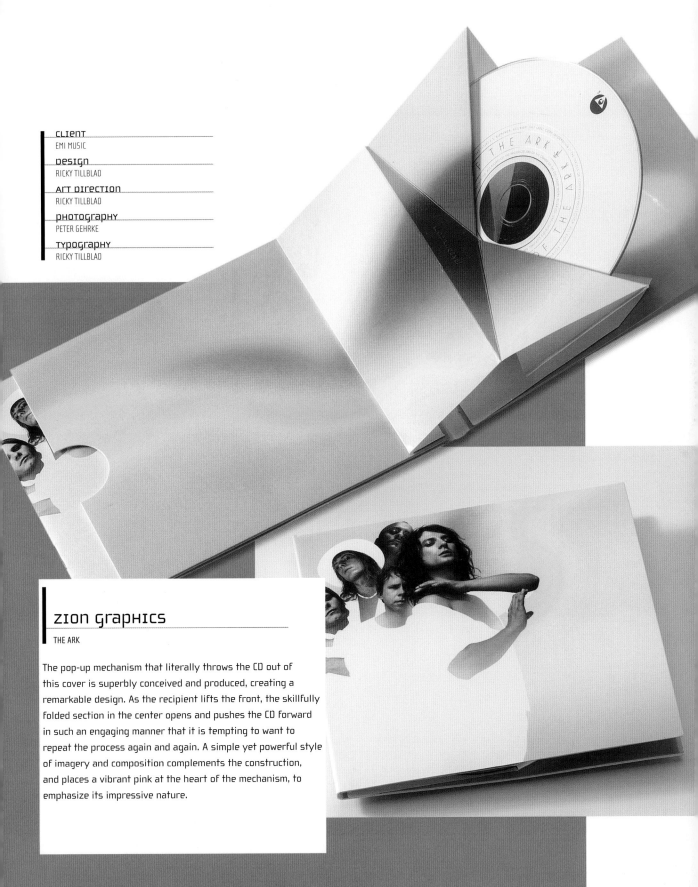

CLIENT
EMI MUSIC

DESIGN
RICKY TILLBLAD

ART DIRECTION
RICKY TILLBLAD

PHOTOGRAPHY
PETER GEHRKE

TYPOGRAPHY
RICKY TILLBLAD

ZION GRAPHICS

THE ARK

The pop-up mechanism that literally throws the CD out of
this cover is superbly conceived and produced, creating a
remarkable design. As the recipient lifts the front, the skillfully
folded section in the center opens and pushes the CD forward
in such an engaging manner that it is tempting to want to
repeat the process again and again. A simple yet powerful style
of imagery and composition complements the construction,
and places a vibrant pink at the heart of the mechanism, to
emphasize its impressive nature.

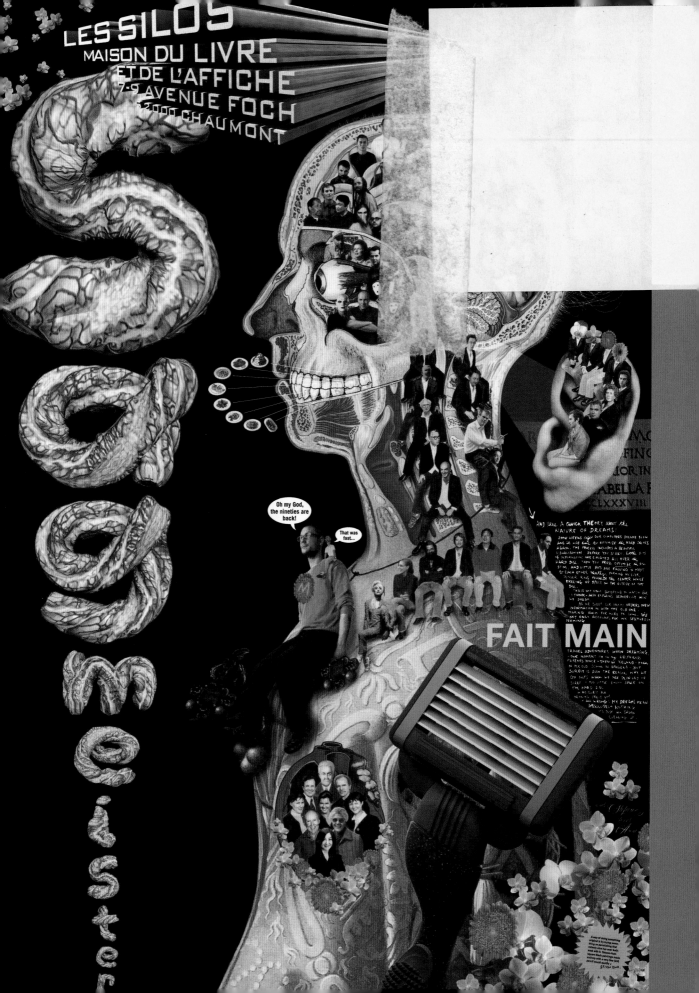

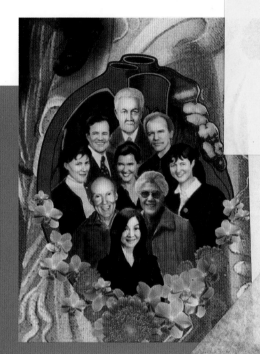

MCE

BERGER
ion
TER
ion
AND GAO MING MAO

sagmeister inc.

CHAUMONT POSTER 1

This striking and rather shocking design by Sagmeister Inc. is for their 2004 exhibit in Chaumont, France. "Our design features all the people who had a significant influence on our work," says art director Stefan Sagmeister, "and whose portraits were hand-painted by tourist illustrators found in New York's Central Park." The poster includes a tremendous amount of fascinating and disturbing detail that rests uncomfortably with the viewer and lingers in the mind's eye. For example, the title lettering appears to be extruded in flesh-like material, and "loved ones" are shown gathered together within a medical illustration of the heart; even more memorably and disconcertingly, dates are carved into Stefan's smile, engendering the involuntary response of tongues being run across front teeth.

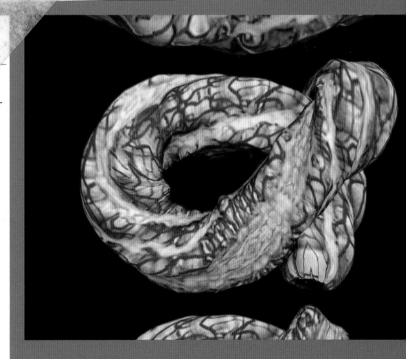

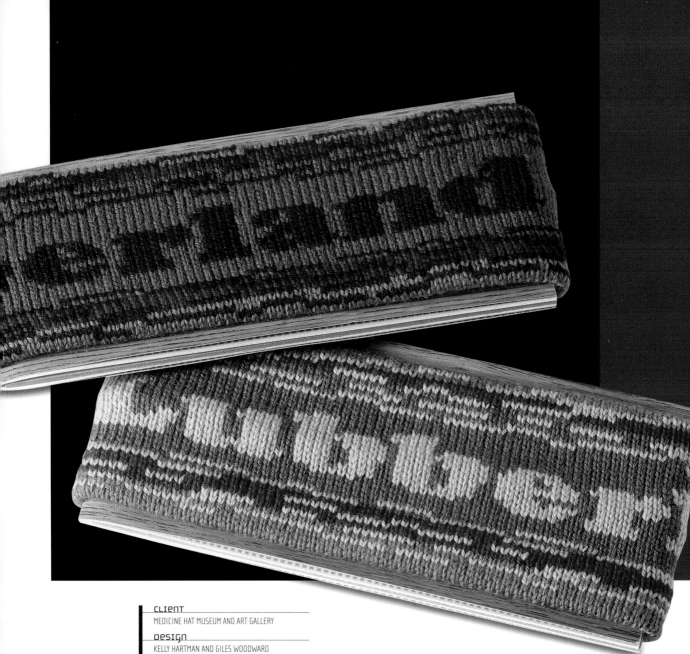

FISHTEN DESIGN

LUANNE MARTINEAU, *LUBBERLAND II*

Lubberland II is the name of Luanne Martineau's exhibition of knitted sculptures; it is consequently very appropriate that her exhibition catalog is impressively enveloped in a personalized knitted headband. Other visual elements, such as printed wood-grain, and a graphic, stitched version of the artist's name, vividly develop the theme, but it is the unexpected use of a headband in a variety of colorways that secures the catalog's individuality and makes it an unforgettable memento of the artist's work.

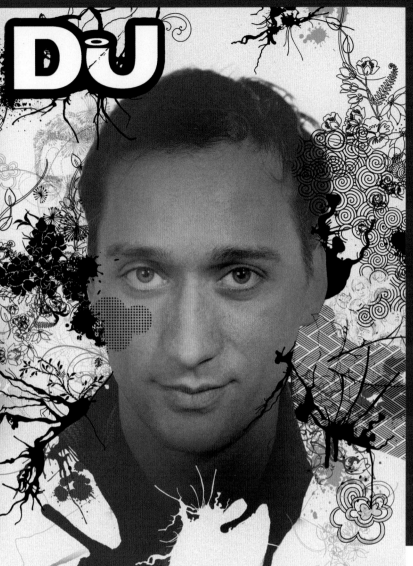

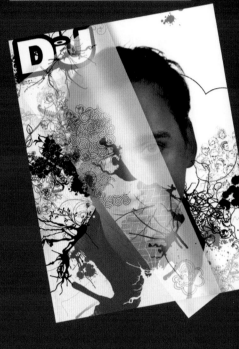

CLIENT
FUTURE PUBLISHING
DESIGN
STEVE PAYNE
ART DIRECTION
OLLY SKINNER
ILLUSTRATION
STEVE PAYNE
PHOTOGRAPHY
MARK OKOH

STUDIO OUTPUT

DJ MAGAZINE "TOP 100 DJS" POLL WINNER COVER

Most magazines do not have a double-layer cover, yet there happen to be two such memorable designs within the pages of *Sticky Graphics*. *DJ* Magazine commissioned Studio Output to design a cover that would partially conceal, and then totally reveal, the identity of the winner of its "Top 100 DJs" poll. This highly mnemonic cover creates an exciting and lingering interactive experience between the illustrated tracing paper layer and the imagery on the cover below, as if inviting readers to enjoy the suspense of this staged disclosure.

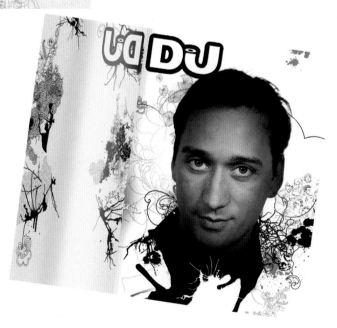

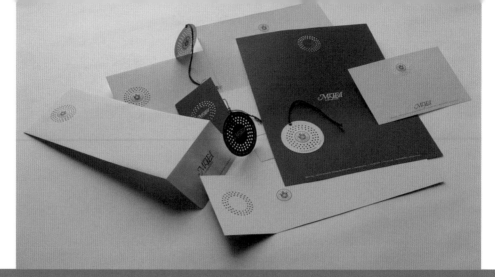

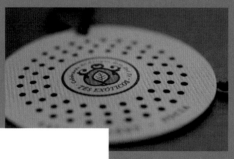
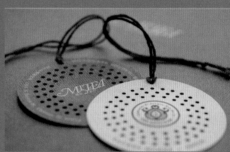

segura inc.

MITEA IDENTITY

Segura Inc. has made clever use of three concentric circles of small die-cut holes to form a surprising and intriguing part of a company identity, and to create a paper version of a tea strainer. Circular swingtags, as well as compliments slips and letterheads, feature this strongly mnemonic device for Mitea, a company focusing on the sale of specialty teas. The design leaves a particularly lasting impression, as business stationery does not often feature such intricate cutting.

CLIENT
MITEA

DESIGN
CARLOS SEGURA

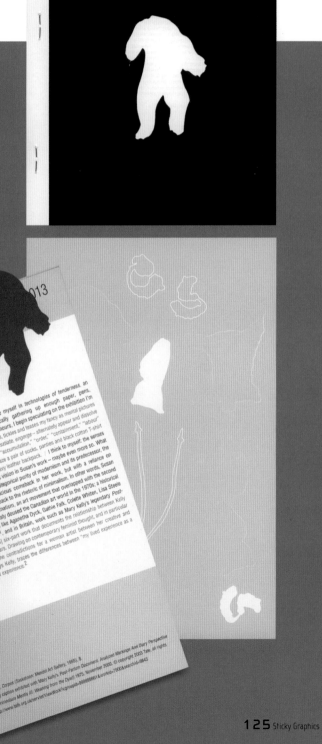

CLIENT
MEDICINE HAT MUSEUM AND ART GALLERY

DESIGN
KELLY HARTMAN AND GILES WOODWARD

ART DIRECTION
KELLY HARTMAN AND GILES WOODWARD

COPYWRITING
SIGRID DAHLE AND JOANNE MARION

PHOTOGRAPHY
RORY MAHONY

TYPOGRAPHY
KELLY HARTMAN AND GILES WOODWARD

FISHTEN DESIGN

SUSAN SHANTZ, *TECHNOLOGIES OF TENDERNESS*

Technologies of Tenderness is a catalog for Susan Shantz's art exhibition, which discusses the interplay of nature and technology at the birth of her son. It immediately arouses interest in the viewer, as a strange fleshy-pink cover, like a child's sticker sheet, wraps the book and provides removable kiss-cut stickers of the artist's work. Curiosity and intrigue are perpetuated by the die-cut of a baby being used as a bookmark. This makes the catalog an essential souvenir that will be remembered for its very uncommon use of materials and processes.

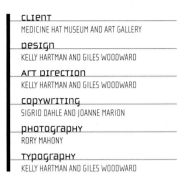

A Long Day's Journey
acute vulnerability

I'm on my way to Medicine Hat, Alberta to immerse myself in technologies of tenderness, an exhibition of work by Susan Shantz. Methodically gathering up enough paper, pens, undergarments, books and toothpaste to last me 36 hours, I begin speculating on the exhibition I'm about to see. The title, technologies of tenderness, tickles and teases my fancy as mental pictures of Susan's earlier bodies of work – hibernaculum, satiate, engorge – alternately appear and dissolve on my mind's screen. The words "abundance," "accumulation," "order," "containment," "labour" and "elegance" spill over one another as I squeeze a pair of socks, panties and black cotton T-shirt into the buttery black compartments of my heavy leather backpack. I think to myself: the senses of touch, taste and smell are as implicated as vision in Susan's work – maybe even more so. What the logocentricism, material austerity and categorical purity of modernism in her work, but with a reliance on Enlightenment, suppressed, stages a delicious comeback in her work, but with a reliance on serialization and repetition that hearkens back to the rhetoric of minimalism. In other words, Susan plays in a dialect informed by post-minimalism, an art movement that overlapped with the second wave of feminism which unceremoniously doused the Canadian art world in the 1970s; a historical juncture that spawned work by artists like Aganetha Dyck, Gathie Falk, Colette Whiten, Lisa Steele and Irene Whittome here in Canada[1], and in Britain, work such as Mary Kelly's legendary Post-Partum Document (1973-79). / [a] six-part work that documents the relationship between Kelly and her son over a period of six years. Drawing on contemporary feminist thought, and in particular on psychoanalysis. It explores the contradictions for a woman artist between her creative and procreative roles. The work, says Kelly, traces the differences between "my lived experience as a mother and my analysis of that experience.2

1 Bruce Grenville, Corpus (Saskatoon: Mendel Art Gallery, 1995), 8.
2 from a display caption exhibited with Mary Kelly's Post-Partum Document, Analyzed Markings And Diary Perspective Schema (Experimentum Mentis III: Weaning from the Dyad) 1975, November 2000. © copyright 2003 Tate, all rights reserved. http://www.tate.org.uk/servlet/ViewWork?cgroupid=999999961&workid=7900&searchid=9843

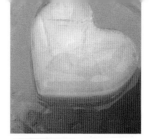

VISUAL FIGURES OF SPEECH

Images and symbols can be used in visual communication in the same way that figures of speech are integrated into spoken or written language—to enrich and expand the communicated message. They are selected and composed with the intention of carrying more than one level of meaning. This not only affects the message, but also tends to make this message more memorable. There are a number of people who lecture and write about developing memory skills; all may have individual approaches, but their basic theories depend on making associations with the information to be memorized, and very often these are visual associations. Similarly, figures of speech used in visual language make links between items in order to heighten meanings, and consequently help them to remain in the viewer's memory.

The simile is the most common figure of speech to be used visually, where two unlike elements are compared or paralleled. "His heart is as cold as ice" is a verbal simile, and it is easy to imagine how this could be depicted visually to convey a person lacking in feeling. It is also interesting to consider how the image is likely to stay in the memory because of its unexpected and unusual nature.

Visual metaphors also make connections between unlikely things, but by substitution. Whatever is pictured will have at least two meanings; when viewed in one way it will appear to have a certain meaning, and when viewed another way it will have an alternative interpretation. The small stakes poster for the wrens on the one hand shows letters that have a linguistic communication for those who understand English, but at the same time carry another meaning, substituting for small, low-nesting birds leaving the long grass (see page 142). In the visual metaphor, there is a sense in which different levels are initially perceived separately, but in the end all levels work together, and create triggers that stimulate the memory.

Metonymy is a very constructive way to simplify a message. Metonymy is a linguistic figure of speech, but it ideally lends itself to use in visual language, whenever a distinctive, well-known image can be utilized to stand for a greater whole. National flags are frequently used metonymically to stand for an entire country; a carefully selected image of a person can be used to indicate the character of everyone in their company. The messages may be a little clichéd, but they are generally easily understood, and are therefore very memorable.

This next section shows examples of work that creatively use various figures of speech to heighten their impact, and make them far more likely to remain in viewers' minds and memories.

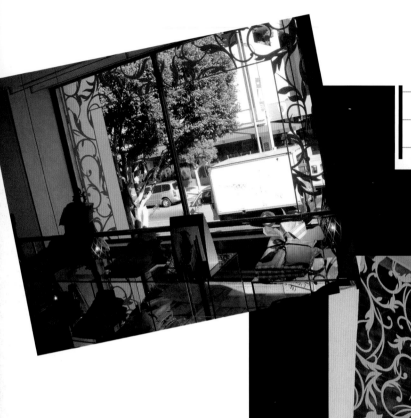

CLIENT
TED BAKER

DESIGN
NICK HAYES

ART DIRECTION
NICK HAYES

IDENTIKAL
TED BAKER CREATIVE SERVICES

TED BAKER, LOS ANGELES

Nick Hayes has created a striking organic pattern,
flowing across the shop front of Ted Baker's store
in Los Angeles; the superbly produced laser-cut
metalwork, painted in white, acts as a visual metaphor
for "distinctive, exclusive, and stylish," not only making
the store stand out from all others in the region,
but also providing a visual universal language that
represents the quality and character of the clothes
that are sold inside. The shop is immediately
recognizable and memorable, and it is perceived
that Ted Baker clothes will be too.

CLIENT
TIME OUT

DESIGN
MICHAEL JOHNSON

ART DIRECTION
MICHAEL JOHNSON

THE REVOLUTION
IS COMING
MARCH 3RD 2004

FREEDOM FOR LONDON

LONDON REPUBLIK

THE REVOLUTION
IS COMING
MARCH 3RD 2004

FREEDOM
FOR
LONDON

LONDON REPUBLIK

johnson banks

LONDON REPUBLIK

How to visualize the relationship between London and the rest of the UK, if London were to be declared a republic, was the challenge set by *Time Out*, and given to Johnson Banks. Dynamic visual metaphors are the company's memorable solution to this challenge; the distinctive shape of the UK landmass is shown made out of cogs, with the "republik of London" and the southeast, being the largest cog, appearing to drive all smaller parts of this mechanism. Another version shown portrays this relationship as a fried egg, with London as the yolk—the nucleus of the country. These fascinating illustrative maps are set against, and contrast with, eye-catching bright red backgrounds, creating an even more dynamic and memorable design.

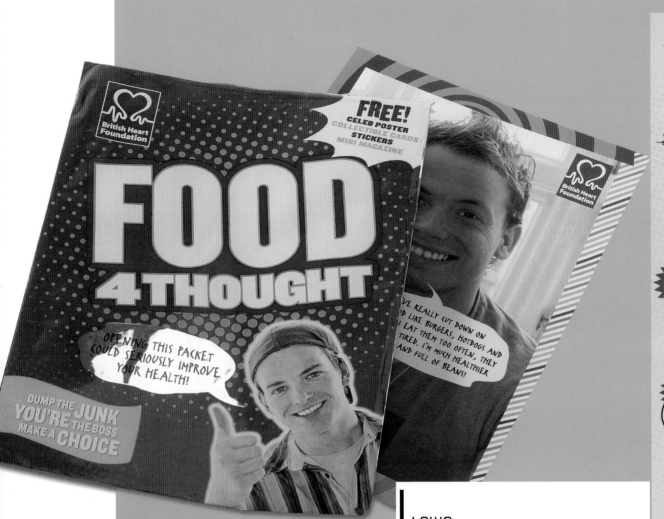

Lowe

FOOD 4 THOUGHT CAMPAIGN

In order to communicate healthy eating issues effectively to 11- and 12-year-olds, the British Heart Foundation chose to use a visual simile created by bright, colorful contemporary approaches that are generally associated with the fast-food industry. "Lookalike" hot-dog sales personnel handed out packs containing a poster, mini-magazine, stickers, and collectible cards; all were styled in "junk food" colors and graphics and placed in a pack made from the same material as fast-food bags. It was only when recipients read the captions, and really looked at the images, that they realized the emphasis of the subject matter. The conflict between the lively visual language and the harsh reality of much of the text and imagery makes this piece both clever and memorable.

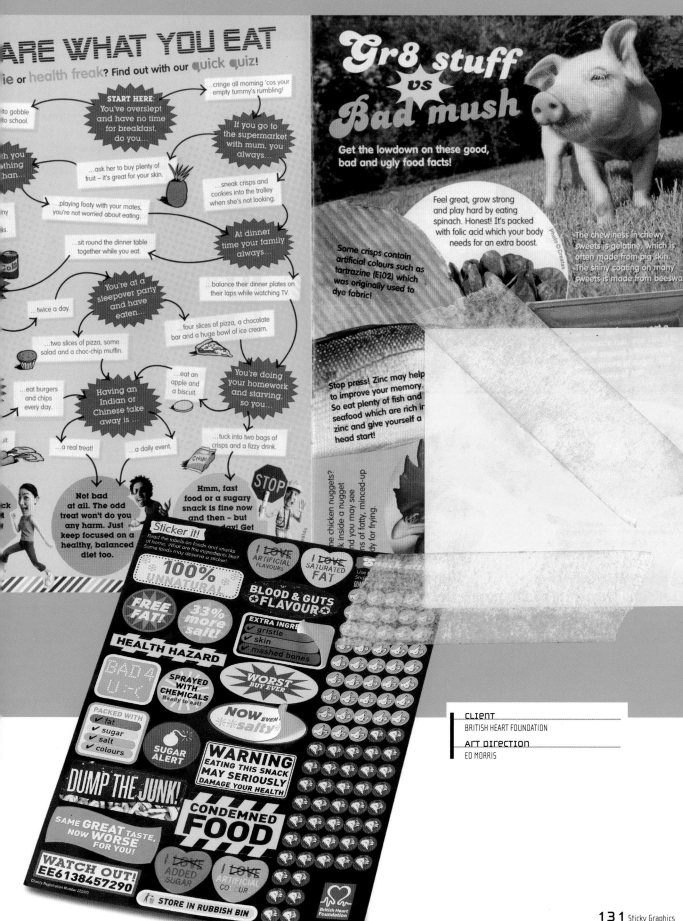

ARE WHAT YOU EAT

...ie or health freak? Find out with our quick quiz!

...to gobble ...to school.

START HERE.
You've overslept and have no time for breakfast, do you...

...cringe all morning 'cos your empty tummy's rumbling!

...ask her to buy plenty of fruit – it's great for your skin.

If you go to the supermarket with mum, you always...

...sneak crisps and cookies into the trolley when she's not looking.

...playing footy with your mates, you're not worried about eating.

...sit round the dinner table together while you eat.

At dinner time your family always...

...balance their dinner plates on their laps while watching TV.

You're at a sleepover party and have eaten...

...twice a day.

...four slices of pizza, a chocolate bar and a huge bowl of ice cream.

...two slices of pizza, some salad and a choc-chip muffin.

...eat an apple and a biscuit.

You're doing your homework and starving, so you...

...eat burgers and chips every day.

Having an Indian or Chinese take away is ...

...a real treat!

...a daily event.

...tuck into two bags of crisps and a fizzy drink.

Not bad at all. The odd treat won't do you any harm. Just keep focused on a healthy, balanced diet too.

Hmm, fast food or a sugary snack is fine now and then – but ...day! Get

STOP

Gr8 stuff vs Bad mush

Get the lowdown on these good, bad and ugly food facts!

Feel great, grow strong and play hard by eating spinach. Honest! It's packed with folic acid which your body needs for an extra boost.

Some crisps contain artificial colours such as tartrazine (E102) which was originally used to dye fabric!

The chewiness in chewy sweets is gelatine, which is often made from pig skin. The shiny coating on many sweets is made from beeswax.

Photo©Creatas

Stop press! Zinc may help to improve your memory. So eat plenty of fish and seafood which are rich in zinc and give yourself a head start!

...e chicken nuggets? ...k inside a nugget ...nd you may see ...s of fatty, minced-up ...dy for frying.

Use ...Snac... DUMP...

Sticker it!
Read the labels on foods and snacks at home. What are the ingredients like? Some foods may deserve a sticker!

I LOVE ARTIFICIAL FLAVOURS

I LOVE SATURATED FAT

100% UNNATURAL

BLOOD & GUTS FLAVOUR

FREE FAT!

33% more salt!

EXTRA INGRE...
✓ gristle
✓ skin
✓ mashed bones

HEALTH HAZARD

BAD 4 U-c

SPRAYED WITH CHEMICALS Ready to eat!

WORST BUY EVER

NOW EVEN saltier

PACKED WITH
✓ fat
✓ sugar
✓ salt
✓ colours

SUGAR ALERT

WARNING EATING THIS SNACK MAY SERIOUSLY DAMAGE YOUR HEALTH

DUMP THE JUNK!

CONDEMNED FOOD

SAME GREAT TASTE, Now WORSE FOR YOU!

I LOVE ADDED SUGAR

I LOVE ARTIFICIAL COLOUR

WATCH OUT! EE6138457290
Charity Registration Number 225971

STORE IN RUBBISH BIN

British Heart Foundation

CLIENT
BRITISH HEART FOUNDATION
ArT Direction
ED MORRIS

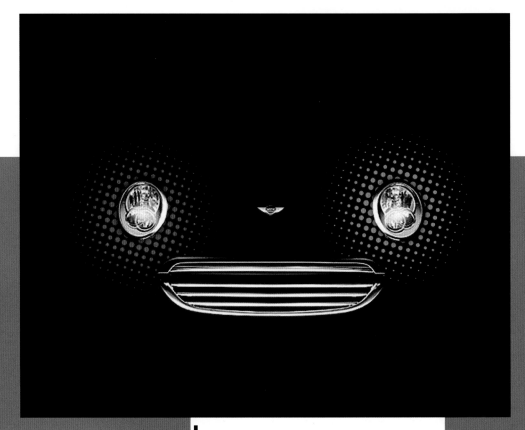

CLIENT
BMW

DESIGN
DOM MURPHY

так!

MINI BMW

Lots of car owners become so attached to their vehicles that they give them names and think of them as having personalities; when looking at the front of their cars, they recognize faces made up from headlights, grills, and hoods. It is exactly this kind of personification that Dom Murphy memorably highlights in his design for BMW Mini; lights, badge, and grill are the only areas of the car that are visible, creating a smiling, friendly face that proves to be a strong mnemonic device, encouraging mini owners and prospective mini owners to remember and think fondly of the little car with the big personality.

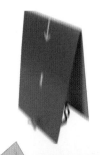

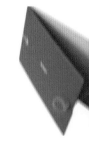

BOING!

BOING! STATIONERY

Imagine the surprise and excitement of opening a card envelope to find that it includes a jumping business card! This is exactly what happens to the recipients of Boing!'s mnemonic promotional piece. This irresistible design is an excellent example of visual simile, as the springing action of the elasticated card simply and memorably replicates the meaning of the Boing! company name. Other items within the stationery set also attempt to echo a springing action. "Unique folds tempt the user to pull apart the opposing arrows visible on folded letterheads, and perpetuate our memorable jumping theme," explains Boing! partner Jeff Leak.

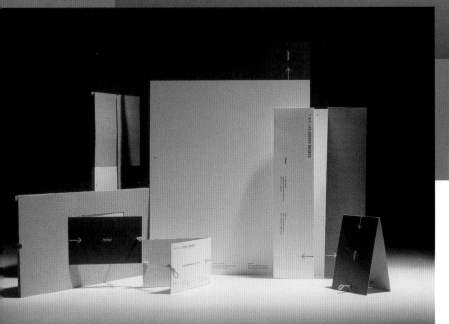

CLIENT
SELF-PROMOTIONAL

DESIGN
JEFF LEAK AND GILES WOODWARD

ART DIRECTION
JEFF LEAK AND GILES WOODWARD

TYPOGRAPHY
JEFF LEAK AND GILES WOODWARD

www.splashinteractive.com

splash
{interactive}

Ivy Wong   t.416.460.0850   ivy@splashinteractive.com

www.splashinteractive.com

splash

www.splashinteractive.com

splash
{interactive}

Ivy Wong   t.416.4

Ivy Wong   t.416.460.0850   ivy@splashinteractive.com

splash interactive

SPLASH INTERACTIVE BUSINESS CARD

Splash is the catchy name of Ivy Wong's design
company in Canada, implying that the work the company
produces creates a visible impact, like the splash
of a stone landing in water. These business cards
memorably develop the simile by using a distinctive
outside shape that references water splashes, sparkly
stock that replicates the glistening of water, and a
fragmented font that is slightly debossed in blue.
"I still get a 'wow' effect every time I hand out this
card," says Ivy Wong, "and it acts like a tiny brochure
that says a lot about what we do." As it is so different
in shape and surface texture from other business
cards, it leaves a lasting impression.

CLIENT
SPLASH INTERACTIVE
DESIGN
IVY WONG
ART DIRECTION
IVY WONG
TYPOGRAPHY
IVY WONG

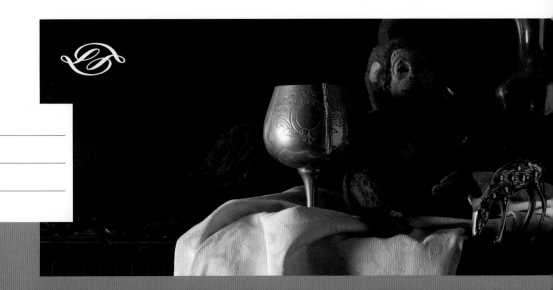

CLIENT
LIZARD LOUNGE

DESIGN
SARA OAKLEY

ART DIRECTION
DAN MOORE

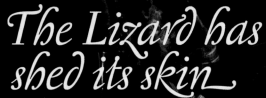

The Lizard has shed its skin

Wednesday, 22nd February 2006

Lizard Lounge

Bar & Nightclub

❋

The newly refurbished Lizard Lounge
is now open as a bar and nightclub.
Champagne cocktails, premium
spirits, Belgian beers, DJs and live
entertainment over three floors.

Strict dress code applies.

❋

Monday – Thursday
Bar; 6pm – 2am
Club; 10pm – 2am

Friday
Bar; 5pm – 3am
Club; 11pm – 3am

Saturday
Bar; 5pm – 3am
Club; 11pm – 3am

❋

Private hire
The Lizard Lounge can accommodate
any size of party, up to 400 people.

For more information call
0115 952 3264.

STUDIO OUTPUT

LIZARD LOUNGE IDENTITY

Studio Output uses visual metaphor in this identity
overhaul for Lizard Lounge in Nottingham, UK. A series
of memorable still-life images, combining a number of
antique items with more contemporary collectibles, was
shot in stately settings, evocative of a seventeenth-
century Dutch painting. It is the compositions and
distinctive chiaroscuro, typical of paintings from this
period, that help the viewer conjure up the feeling
that Lizard Lounge is a place of luxury, wealth, and
unashamed decadence. The images stand for a style
and atmosphere that will be experienced in the
nightclub, and are particularly significant because
they are not typical of many club environments.

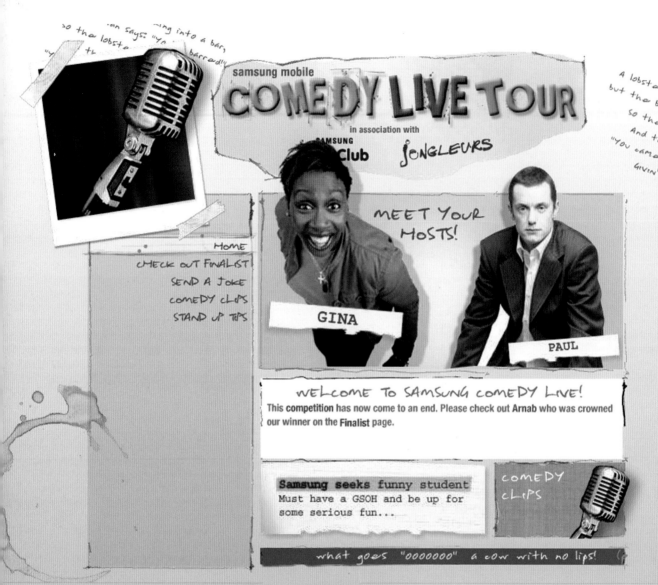

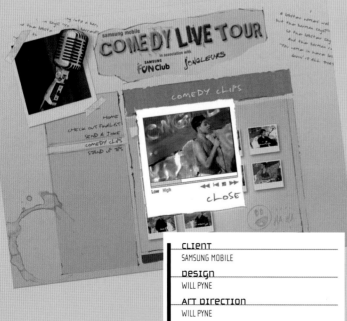

HOLLer

SAMSUNG COMEDY LIVE WEB SITE

The Samsung Comedy Live Web site is distinctive, and sticks in viewers' memories, because it harnesses a range of unusual and unexpected visual elements. Instead of displaying sophisticated, technical imagery, skillfully created through specialist software programs, the site appears to be made up of handwriting, torn paper and masking tape, polaroid shots, and coffee mug stains. It is also intriguing, because the imagery acts as a visual metaphor for the business of live comedy, creating a visual interpretation that represents the real-life experiences that inspire and in turn construct stand-up comedy. The synergy between style and subject matter also gives the design poignancy and therefore memorability.

CLIENT
SAMSUNG MOBILE

DESIGN
WILL PYNE

ART DIRECTION
WILL PYNE

ILLUSTRATION
TOM HASWELL

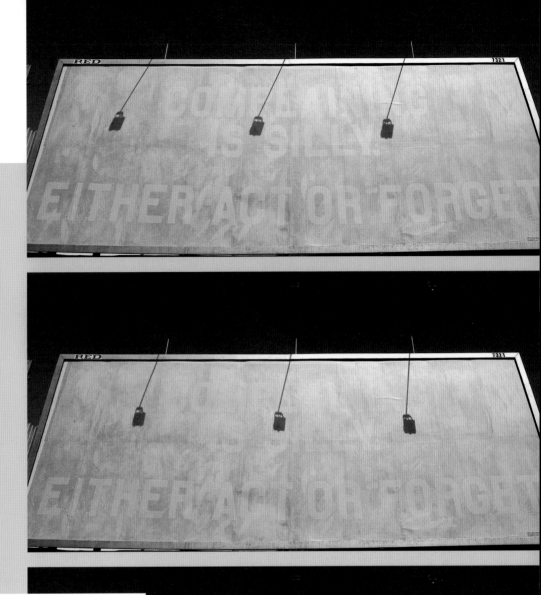

sagmeister inc.

Sagmeister Inc. has created a fascinating and memorable visual simile as a billboard design for the Experimenta in Lisbon. "The poster was made out of newsprint paper, in order to take advantage of the fact that newsprint yellows significantly in the sun, and we made a giant stencil so that we could expose the paper to sunlight," says Stefan Sagmeister. "After a week, it spelled out in white on a dark yellowed background, 'Complaining is silly. Either act or forget.' We then shipped the exposed newsprint to Lisbon, and through further exposure there, the typography and the complaining slowly faded away," he concludes. Pertinent use of photochromic effects caused this poster to steadily change throughout its lifespan, and this fact makes it remarkable and enduring.

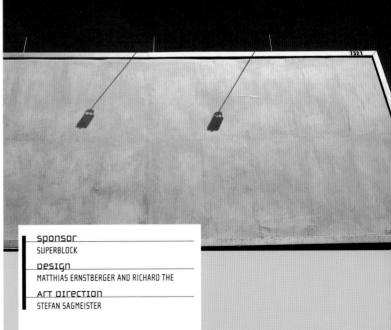

sponsor
SUPERBLOCK

Design
MATTHIAS ERNSTBERGER AND RICHARD THE

Art Direction
STEFAN SAGMEISTER

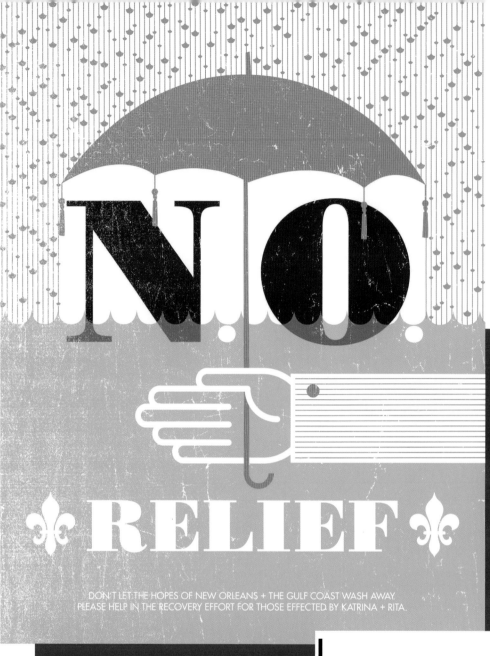

CHRIS RUBINO

N.O. RELIEF

"Double entendre is used to give this poster its memorable character," says Chris Rubino of his design for 25 Above Water. "My design simply states the situation in the Gulf coast during the fall of 2005—N.O. stands for New Orleans, but at the same time can be read as 'no,'" he concludes. The memorability is enhanced because the letters are also used metaphorically, as replacements for the people of New Orleans, standing partially submerged in the flood waters, and ironically protected by a fragile, pink, tasselled parasol.

CLIENT
25 ABOVE WATER

DESIGN
CHRIS RUBINO

ART DIRECTION
CHRIS RUBINO

ILLUSTRATION
CHRIS RUBINO

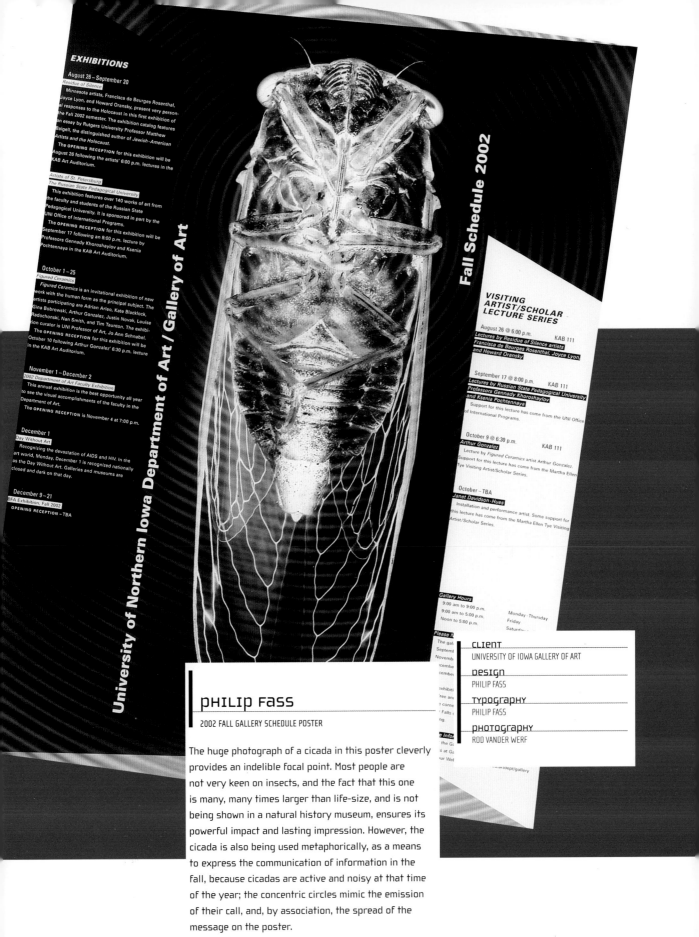

PHILIP FASS

2002 FALL GALLERY SCHEDULE POSTER

The huge photograph of a cicada in this poster cleverly provides an indelible focal point. Most people are not very keen on insects, and the fact that this one is many, many times larger than life-size, and is not being shown in a natural history museum, ensures its powerful impact and lasting impression. However, the cicada is also being used metaphorically, as a means to express the communication of information in the fall, because cicadas are active and noisy at that time of the year; the concentric circles mimic the emission of their call, and, by association, the spread of the message on the poster.

CLIENT
UNIVERSITY OF IOWA GALLERY OF ART

DESIGN
PHILIP FASS

TYPOGRAPHY
PHILIP FASS

PHOTOGRAPHY
ROD VANDER WERF

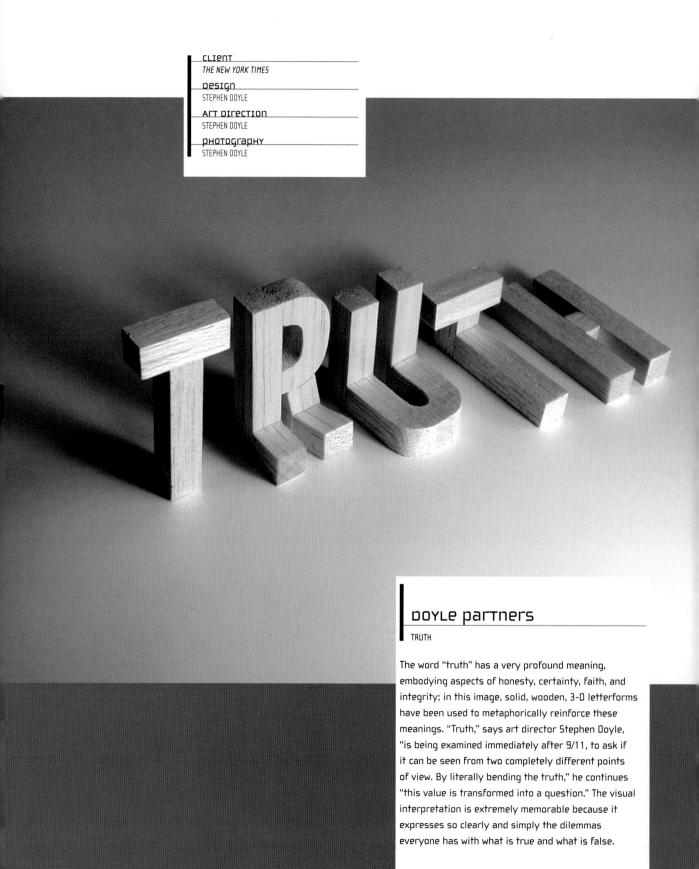

CLIENT
THE NEW YORK TIMES

DESIGN
STEPHEN DOYLE

ART DIRECTION
STEPHEN DOYLE

PHOTOGRAPHY
STEPHEN DOYLE

DOYLE PARTNERS

TRUTH

The word "truth" has a very profound meaning, embodying aspects of honesty, certainty, faith, and integrity; in this image, solid, wooden, 3-D letterforms have been used to metaphorically reinforce these meanings. "Truth," says art director Stephen Doyle, "is being examined immediately after 9/11, to ask if it can be seen from two completely different points of view. By literally bending the truth," he continues "this value is transformed into a question." The visual interpretation is extremely memorable because it expresses so clearly and simply the dilemmas everyone has with what is true and what is false.

CLIENT
TED BAKER

DESIGN
MARK CAYLOR

ART DIRECTION
ROB O'CONNOR AND MARK CAYLOR

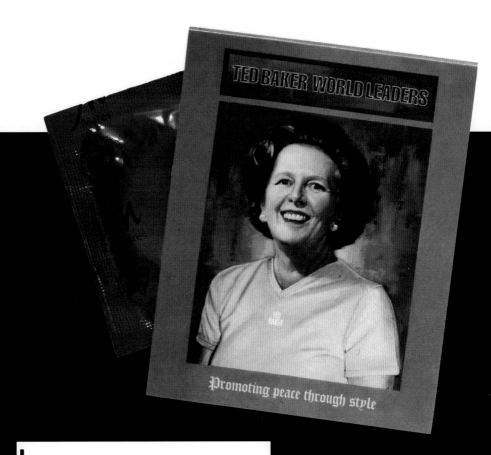

STYLOrouge

TED BAKER WORLD LEADER CONDOMS

The fashion company Ted Baker is renowned for its distinctive and often quirky outlook on life. Stylorouge has perpetuated this view, with an amusing and memorable design for promotional world leader condoms. The Margaret Thatcher version is shown here. It displays an image of a smiling "iron lady" sporting a Ted Baker T-shirt with the strapline "promoting peace through style." This tongue-in-cheek send-up of Britain's first and only female prime minister to date brings a smile to the face of the viewer. It is amusing enough to imagine Margaret Thatcher wearing T-shirts, let alone personally promoting peace, harmony, and style through safe sex.

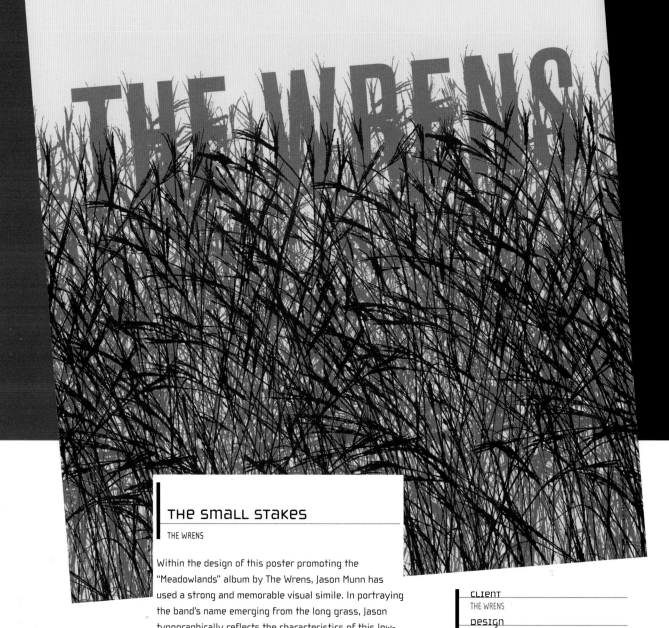

DECEMBER 2
PARCHMAN FARM • THE DECORATION
SLIM'S

THE WRENS

THE SMALL STAKES

THE WRENS

Within the design of this poster promoting the
"Meadowlands" album by The Wrens, Jason Munn has
used a strong and memorable visual simile. In portraying
the band's name emerging from the long grass, Jason
typographically reflects the characteristics of this low-
nesting bird. "The band has been around for many years,
but has only just started to get recognized," says Jason,
"so I wanted this emergence to come across in the type."

CLIENT
THE WRENS
DESIGN
JASON MUNN

blur

CLIENT
EMI MUSIC
DESIGN
STYLOROUGE
ART DIRECTION
ROB O'CONNOR

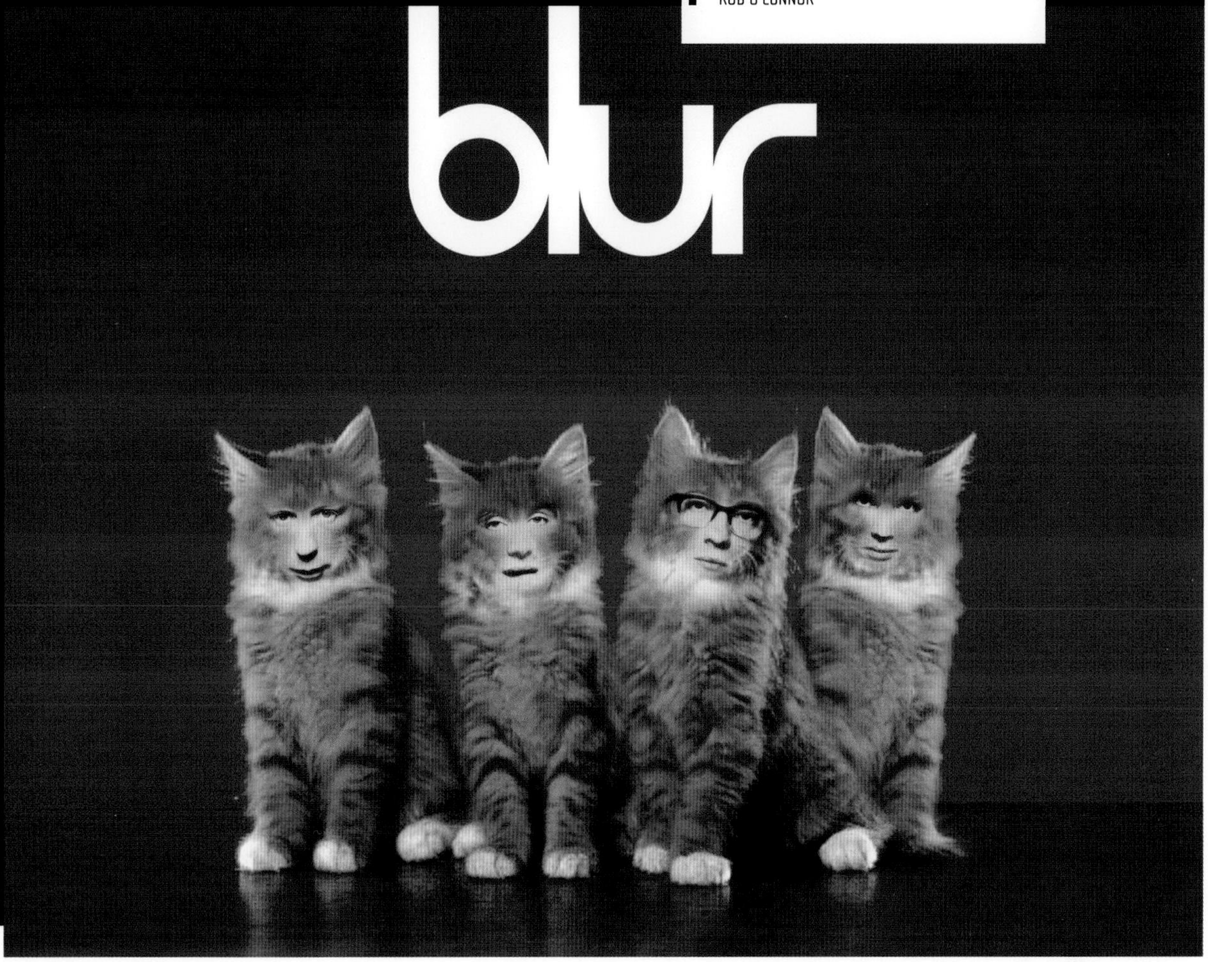

STYLOROUGE

BEST OF BLUR ALBUM SLEEVE PROPOSAL

This eye-catching Stylorouge design uses visual simile; members of the British band Blur are likened to cuddly, soft kittens. Rob O'Connor's haunting image brings together the gentle nature of four cute felines with the loud, forceful characters of the band members, creating a surprising, unexpected, and unforgettable image.

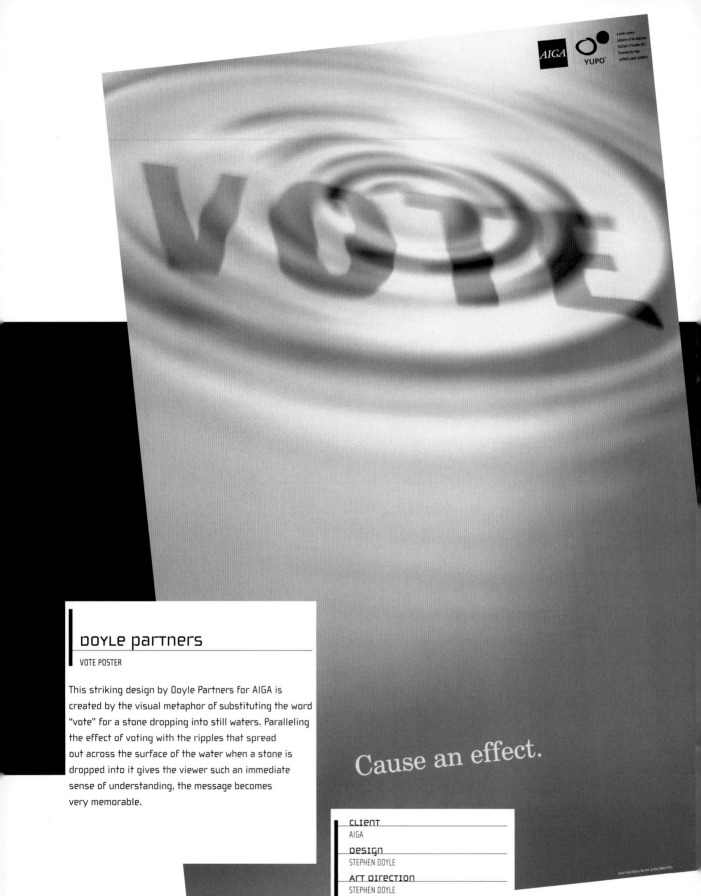

A public service
initiative of the American
Institute of Graphic Arts.
Presented by Yupo
synthetic paper products.

DOYLE Partners

VOTE POSTER

This striking design by Doyle Partners for AIGA is
created by the visual metaphor of substituting the word
"vote" for a stone dropping into still waters. Paralleling
the effect of voting with the ripples that spread
out across the surface of the water when a stone is
dropped into it gives the viewer such an immediate
sense of understanding, the message becomes
very memorable.

Cause an effect.

CLIENT
AIGA

DESIGN
STEPHEN DOYLE

ART DIRECTION
STEPHEN DOYLE

PHOTOGRAPHY
STEPHEN DOYLE

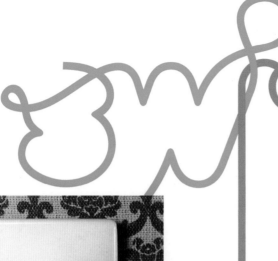

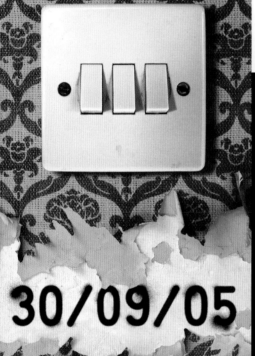

30/09/05

client
MINISTRY OF SOUND, LONDON
Design
STEVE PAYNE AND DAN MOORE
Art Direction
ROB COKE

STUDIO OUTPUT

SWITCH

"The publicity for 'Switch' had to convey excitement, and what better way to symbolize an electric atmosphere than with a logo and design inspired by the UK electrical system," says Rob Coke of Studio Output. This visual and verbal pun on the word "switch" and its "wiring" interpretation, as well as its light switch context, provides a number of interacting levels of meaning that not only hold the viewer's attention but also inject a vitality that makes the layout memorable.

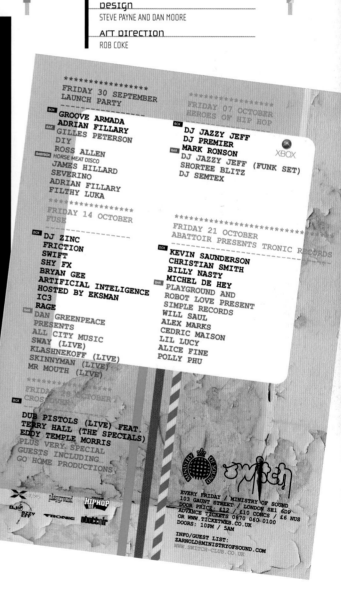

FRIDAY 30 SEPTEMBER
LAUNCH PARTY
BOX **GROOVE ARMADA**
ADRIAN FILLARY
BAR GILLES PETERSON
DIY
ROSS ALLEN
BABYBOX HORSE MEAT DISCO
JAMES HILLARD
SEVERINO
ADRIAN FILLARY
FILTHY LUKA

FRIDAY 14 OCTOBER
FUSE

BOX DJ ZINC
FRICTION
SWIFT
SHY FX
BRYAN GEE
ARTIFICIAL INTELIGENCE
HOSTED BY EKSMAN
IC3
RAGE
BAR DAN GREENPEACE
PRESENTS
ALL CITY MUSIC
SWAY (LIVE)
KLASHNEKOFF (LIVE)
SKINNYMAN (LIVE)
MR MOUTH (LIVE)

FRIDAY 28 OCTOBER
CROSSOVER
BOX DUB PISTOLS (LIVE) FEAT.
TERRY HALL (THE SPECIALS)
EDDY TEMPLE MORRIS
PLUS VERY SPECIAL
GUESTS INCLUDING
GO HOME PRODUCTIONS

FRIDAY 07 OCTOBER
HEROES OF HIP HOP

BOX **DJ JAZZY JEFF**
DJ PREMIER
MARK RONSON
BAR DJ JAZZY JEFF (FUNK SET)
SHORTEE BLITZ
DJ SEMTEX

FRIDAY 21 OCTOBER
ABATTOIR PRESENTS TRONIC RECORDS

BOX **KEVIN SAUNDERSON**
CHRISTIAN SMITH
BILLY NASTY
MICHEL DE HEY
BAR PLAYGROUND AND
ROBOT LOVE PRESENT
SIMPLE RECORDS
WILL SAUL
ALEX MARKS
CEDRIC MAISON
LIL LUCY
ALICE FINE
POLLY PHU

EVERY FRIDAY / MINISTRY OF SOUND
103 GAUNT STREET / LONDON SE1 6DP
DOOR PRICE: £12 / £10 CONCS / £6 NUS
ADVANCE TICKETS 0870 060 0100
OR WWW.TICKETWEB.CO.UK
DOORS: 10PM / 5AM

INFO/GUEST LIST:
ZARNOLD@MINISTRYOFSOUND.COM
WWW.SWITCH-CLUB.CO.UK

CLIENT
MTV SINGAPORE

DESIGN
REX ADVINCULA AND JOYCE TAI

ART DIRECTION
REX ADVINCULA AND JOYCE TAI

ILLUSTRATION
REX ADVINCULA AND JOYCE TAI

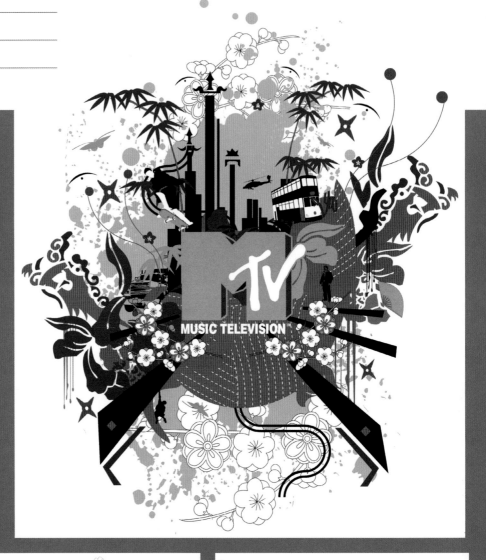

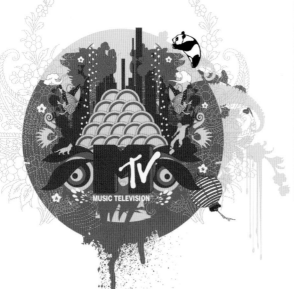

Inksurge

MTV SINGAPORE LOGOS

These memorable logos for MTV make striking use of visual metonymy. Rex and Joyce, of Philippine design company Inksurge, have firmly positioned MTV as a part of Asian culture by selecting and using representative images in a culturally significant style that stand for Asia as a whole.

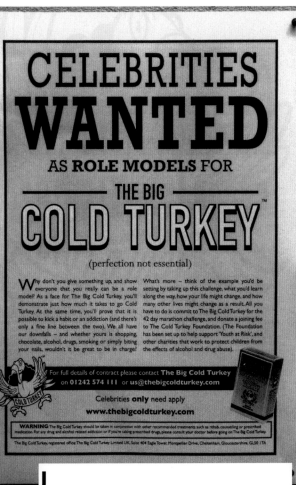

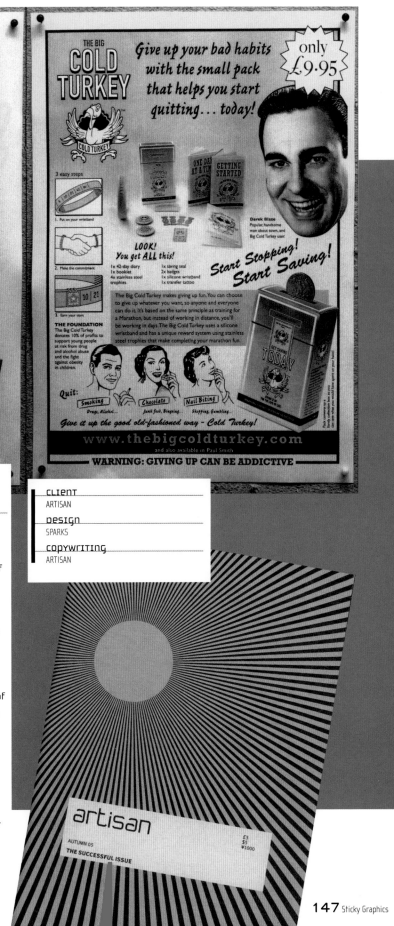

sparks

ARTISAN JOURNAL

The fall 2005 publication of *Artisan* is entitled "The Successful Issue." It uses a number of visual figures of speech to convey its messages in thought-provoking, memorable visual language. The cover, printed in gold and rich blue, emulates a golden sun with glistening rays, embodying all the familiar metaphors relating to success: "the sun shines out of their eyes," "born on the sunny side of the street," and "the sun shines on the righteous." Inside, a particularly striking spread consists of two retro-styled posters, one in the form of a Wild West "wanted" notice, and the other embracing the 1950s characteristics of line drawings, cutout images, typefaces, and tints. Both make a lasting impression on readers because the relationships between design styles and design content are unexpected and somewhat uneasy; the design styles attract attention and provide certain associations that on closer inspection become visual metaphors for combating different addictions and temptations.

CLIENT
ARTISAN

DESIGN
SPARKS

COPYWRITING
ARTISAN

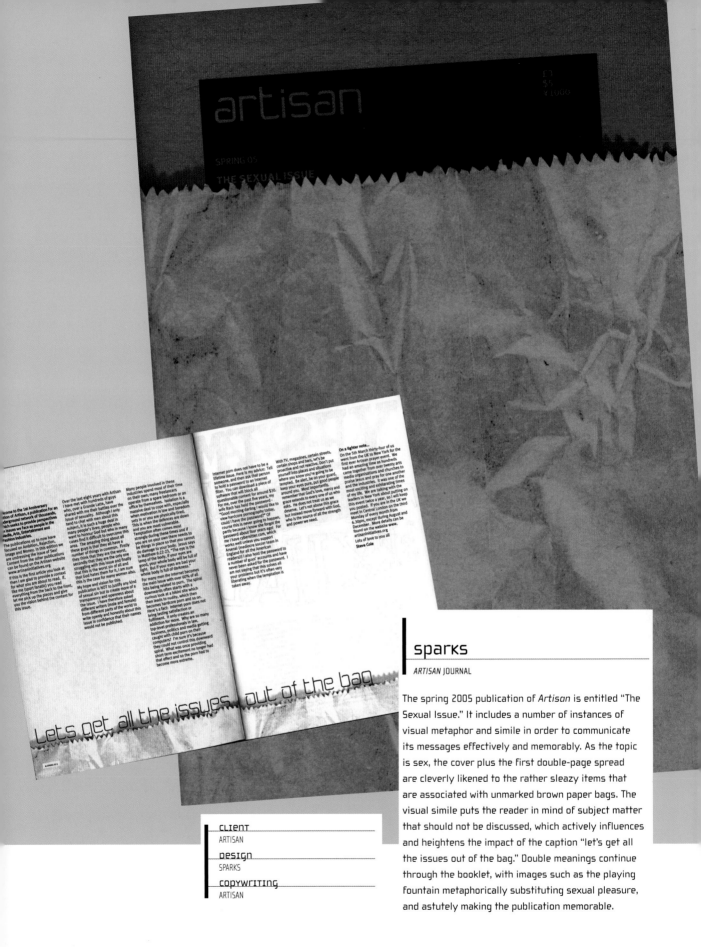

sparks

ARTISAN JOURNAL

The spring 2005 publication of *Artisan* is entitled "The Sexual Issue." It includes a number of instances of visual metaphor and simile in order to communicate its messages effectively and memorably. As the topic is sex, the cover plus the first double-page spread are cleverly likened to the rather sleazy items that are associated with unmarked brown paper bags. The visual simile puts the reader in mind of subject matter that should not be discussed, which actively influences and heightens the impact of the caption "let's get all the issues out of the bag." Double meanings continue through the booklet, with images such as the playing fountain metaphorically substituting sexual pleasure, and astutely making the publication memorable.

CLIENT
ARTISAN

DESIGN
SPARKS

COPYWRITING
ARTISAN

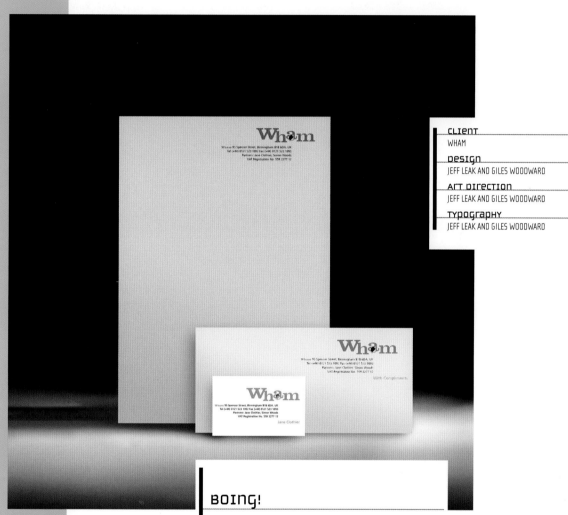

BOING!

WHAM STATIONERY

Boing! has created a memorable visual metaphor as
the namestyle for arts marketing company Wham. The
striking concept behind this mark incorporates a bullet
hole. This symbolizes the organization's main activity,
which is "target marketing!" It is this realistic gunshot
effect, drilled through the bowl of the letter "a" within
each item of stationery, which is such a successful way
of fixing Wham in the viewer's mind.

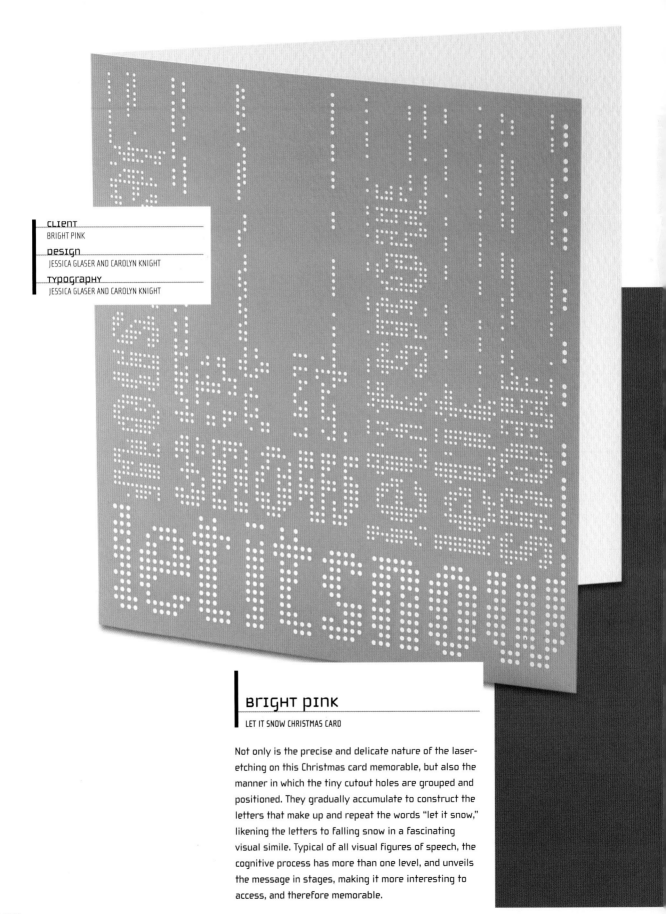

CLIENT
BRIGHT PINK

DESIGN
JESSICA GLASER AND CAROLYN KNIGHT

TYPOGRAPHY
JESSICA GLASER AND CAROLYN KNIGHT

BRIGHT PINK

LET IT SNOW CHRISTMAS CARD

Not only is the precise and delicate nature of the laser-
etching on this Christmas card memorable, but also the
manner in which the tiny cutout holes are grouped and
positioned. They gradually accumulate to construct the
letters that make up and repeat the words "let it snow,"
likening the letters to falling snow in a fascinating
visual simile. Typical of all visual figures of speech, the
cognitive process has more than one level, and unveils
the message in stages, making it more interesting to
access, and therefore memorable.

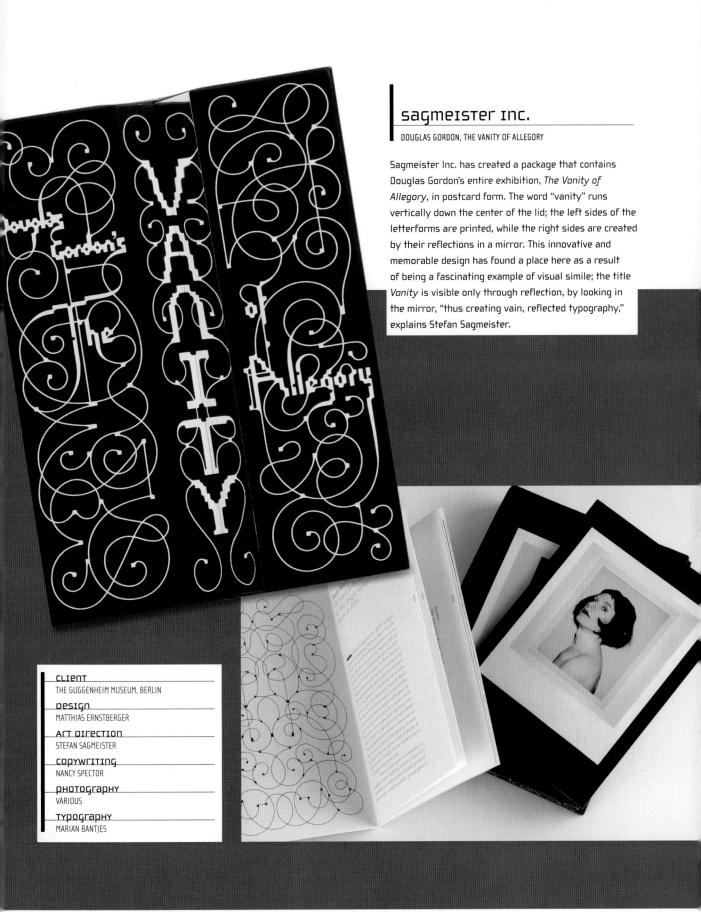

sagmeister inc.

DOUGLAS GORDON, THE VANITY OF ALLEGORY

Sagmeister Inc. has created a package that contains Douglas Gordon's entire exhibition, *The Vanity of Allegory*, in postcard form. The word "vanity" runs vertically down the center of the lid; the left sides of the letterforms are printed, while the right sides are created by their reflections in a mirror. This innovative and memorable design has found a place here as a result of being a fascinating example of visual simile; the title *Vanity* is visible only through reflection, by looking in the mirror, "thus creating vain, reflected typography," explains Stefan Sagmeister.

CLIENT
THE GUGGENHEIM MUSEUM, BERLIN

DESIGN
MATTHIAS ERNSTBERGER

ART DIRECTION
STEFAN SAGMEISTER

COPYWRITING
NANCY SPECTOR

PHOTOGRAPHY
VARIOUS

TYPOGRAPHY
MARIAN BANTJES

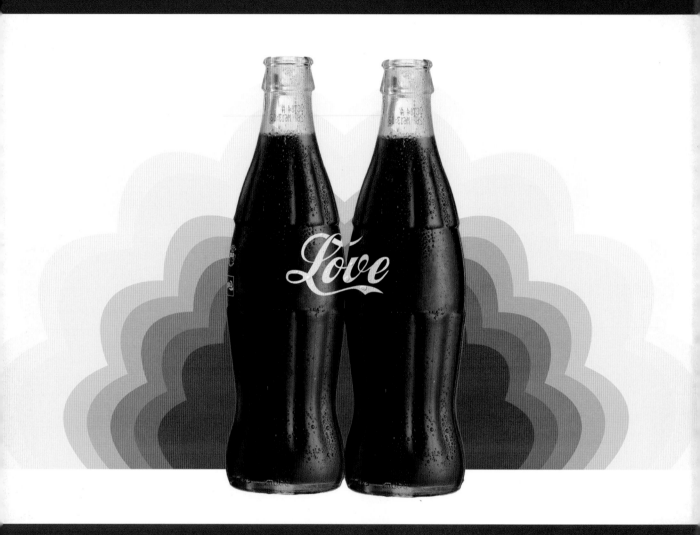

CLIENT	
COCA-COLA	
DESIGN	
COCA-COLA	
ART DIRECTION	
YAN, LUKE, MOTHER	
COPYWRITING	
YAN, LUKE, MOTHER	
ILLUSTRATION	
AIRSIDE	

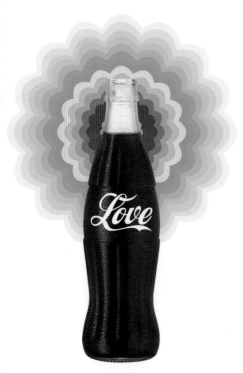

Airside

COCA-COLA

The Coca-Cola bottle must be one of the most mnemonic shapes in the world, and its distinctive, flowing namestyle is recognized and remembered by almost everyone. Airside has created a series of extremely eye-catching posters for Coca-Cola that dynamically present the bottles with brightly colored halos. These become particularly memorable pieces of design, because instead of saying "Coca Cola," the familiar curvy white lettering says "Love." At first, most viewers do not notice the typographic change, which not only creates a design surprise, but also lies at the core of powerful visual metonymy. It is as if the lettering, colors, and background illustrative elements stand for the whole spectrum of love, peace, and harmony associated with this brand over many decades. The subsequent response gives a sense of enjoyment and satisfaction and makes the posters highly memorable. The selected double-page spreads are highlighted because they make such dynamic use of color, image, and composition, that they are bound to make a lasting impression on readers.

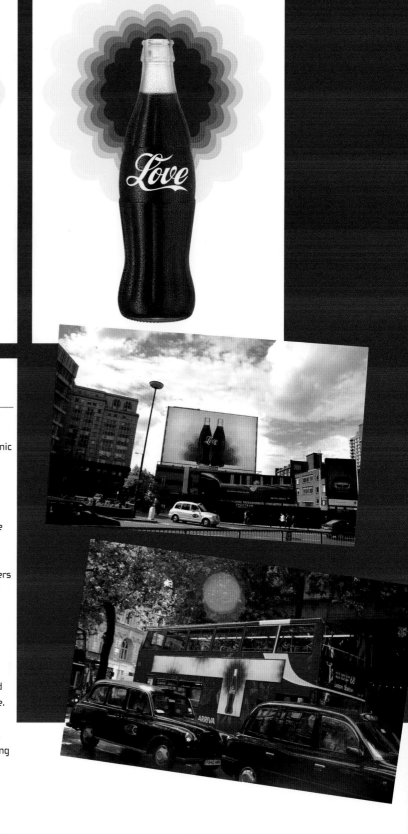

INDEX

Directory

CHRIS RUBINO
102 JACKSON STREET, BROOKLYN, NY 11211, USA

CLEAR MAGAZINE
433 NORTH WASHINGTON, ROYAL OAK, MI 48067, USA

DIRK RUDOLPH
PRINZ REGENT STRASSE 50-60, BOCHUM 44795, GERMANY

DOYLE PARTNERS
1123 BROADWAY, NEW YORK, NY 10010, USA

FISHTEN DESIGN
2203 32ND AVENUE SOUTH WEST, CALGARY,
ALBERTA, T2T 1X2, CANADA

FORM FÜNF BREMEN
GRAF MOLTKE STRASSE 7, BREMEM 28203, GERMANY

HALLO!
15 DORAN CLOSE, HALESOWEN, WEST MIDLANDS, B63 1JZ, UK

HOLLER
13–19 VINE HILL, CLERKENWELL, LONDON, EC1R 5DW, UK

IDENTIKAL
STUDIO 25, 217 EAST 22ND STREET, NEW YORK, NY 10010,
USA

INKSURGE
171 CORDILLERA STREET, STA. MESA HTS, QUEZON CITY, 1100,
PHILIPPINES

33 RPM
105 HARVARD AVENUE EAST #301, SEATTLE, WA 98102, USA

AIRSIDE
24 CROSS STREET, LONDON, N1 2BG, UK

BANKERWESSEL
SKEPPSBRON 10, STOCKHOLM 111 30, SWEDEN

BOING!
47 RODEN AVENUE, KIDDERMINSTER,
WORCESTERSHIRE, DY10 2RE, UK

BRIGHT PINK COMMUNICATIONS DESIGN
LAPLEY STUDIO, LAPLEY, STAFFORD, ST19 9JS, UK

BRITISH HEART FOUNDATION
14 FITZHARDINGE STREET, LONDON, W1H 6DH, UK

CADBURY SCHWEPPES PLC
FRANKLIN HOUSE, BOURNVILLE LANE, BOURNVILLE,
BIRMINGHAM, B30 2NB, UK

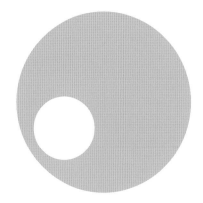

Rebecca Foster Design
54 CASSIOBURY ROAD, LONDON, E17 7JF, UK

Rinzen
PO BOX 1729, NEW FARM, BRISBANE, QLD 4003, AUSTRALIA

Sagmeister Inc.
222 WEST 14 STREET, NEW YORK, NY 10011, USA

SEA Design
70 ST. JOHN STREET, LONDON EC1M 4DT, UK

Segura Inc.
1110 NORTH MILWAUKEE AVENUE, CHICAGO, IL 60622-4017, USA

Slang
WICHERT STRASSE 54, BERLIN 10439, GERMANY

Snap-e-chuck
5205 NORTH WEST 33 AVENUE, FORT LAUDERDALE, FL 33309, USA

Sparks
4–6 DRYDEN STREET, LONDON, WC2E 9NH, UK

Splash Interactive
1103–33 BLOOR STREET EAST, TORONTO, ONTARIO, M4W 3H1, CANADA

Studio Output
2 BROADWAY, LACE MARKET, NOTTINGHAM, NG1 1PS, UK

Stylorouge
57–60 CHARLOTTE ROAD, LONDON, EC2A 3QT, UK

TAK!
118 THE CUSTARD FACTORY, GIBB STREET, BIRMINGHAM, B9 4AA, UK

Taxi Studio Ltd
93 PRINCESS VICTORIA STREET, CLIFTON, BRISTOL, BS8 4DD, UK

Taylors of Harrogate
PLUMPTON PARK, HARROGATE, NORTH YORKSHIRE, HG3 1EF, UK

Thames & Hudson
181A HIGH HOLBORN, LONDON, WC1V 7QX, UK

The Partners
ALBION COURTYARD, GREENHILL RENTS, LONDON, EC1M 6PQ, UK

The Small Stakes
1847 FIFTH AVENUE, OAKLAND, CA 94606, USA

344 Design
10 N. GRAND AVENUE, SUITE 7 PASADENA, CA 91103, USA

Twelve20
20 SHERWOOD ROAD, SMETHWICK, WEST MIDLANDS, B67 5DE, UK

White Stuff
TUBORG HOUSE, MANDRELL ROAD, LONDON, SW2 5DL, UK

Wuffdesign
KAISER STRASSE 69, FRANKFURT AM MAIN 60329, GERMANY

Zion Graphics
BELLMANSGATAN 8, STOCKHOLM 118 20, SWEDEN

THE AUTHORS

Carolyn Knight and Jessica Glaser are partners at the design firm Bright Pink. Their clients come from areas including building and property, charities, textiles, horticulture, education, and healthcare. Both authors are art and design lecturers, and live in the UK.

The authors have also written and designed *Create Impact With Type, Image, and Color* for RotoVision, as well as *Layout: Making it Fit* published by Rockport.